We acknowledge the Traditional Owners and Custodians of the land on which we live, work, surf, play and create. We recognise their continuing connection to the land and waters, and thank them for protecting this coastline and its ecosystems since time immemorial. We pay our respects to Elders past and present, and extend that respect to all First Nation people today.

SURF—LIFE

WOMEN WHO LIVE TO SURF AND CREATE

Words by Gill Hutchison
Photos by Willem-Dirk du Toit

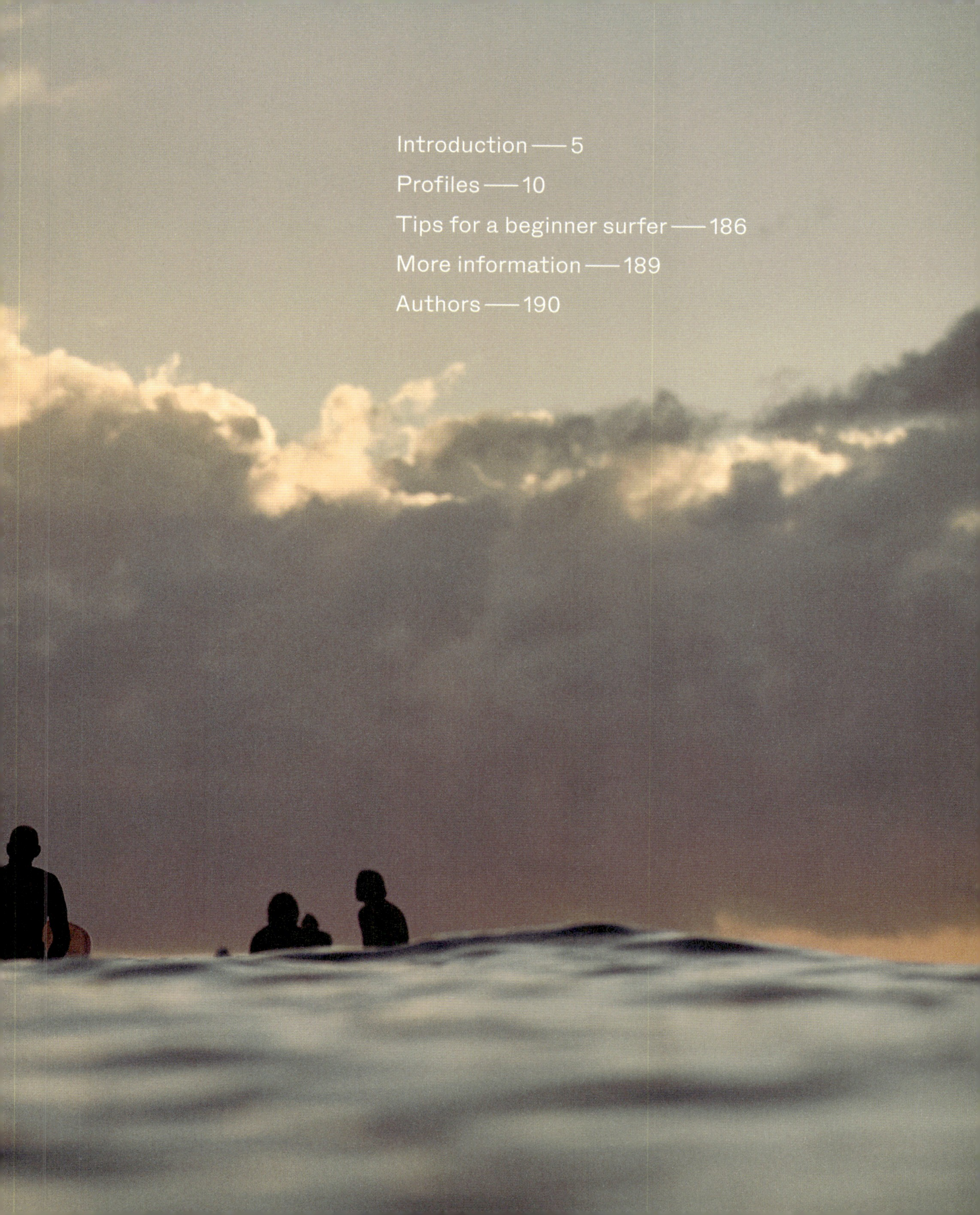

Introduction

Surfing is hard. There isn't a single surfer who isn't always striving for something more – a better turn, a different board, the next perfect ride – just beyond reach. As grasping and frustrating as surfing can feel for the beginner, or even for the seasoned rider, it is a salve for the soul like no other. The connection with nature, the suspension of time as an unbroken wave rolls beneath you, the unpredictability of the conditions, and the waxing and waning of people in the line-up: all of these constantly shifting elements keep surfing interesting and addictive.

To an outsider, surfers' behaviour can appear a little odd. What exactly are they looking at when they stand, arms crossed, staring out to sea for an inordinate amount of time? Why is everyone so at ease nearly naked in the carpark when changing into their wetsuits? And why are some surfers compelled to run down the beach to the waves? What's wrong with a casual stroll enjoying the surroundings?

Every line-up has its own ecosystem of characters. It's not just the waves you learn to read but the faces, too. If you surf regularly at the same spot there can be a mystique surrounding some of the people you surf with. You may know their car, their board, their surfing style and whether they've been on a surf trip that year. Everything but their name. Or what they do for work. Would you recognise them if you bumped into them on land? Perhaps not. Yet there's a unique bond and the camaraderie and casual chats in the carpark are just as important as surfing itself.

Unfortunately for some surfing culture can feel exclusive and prejudiced. Throughout surfing history women have been marginalised and largely ignored. There have been Australian trailblazers such as Isabel Letham in the early 20th century, who was one of the first Australians to ride a surfboard. Gail Couper has the unbeatable record of winning ten Bells Beach surfing titles during the 60s and 70s. Pauline Menczer mostly self-funded her world surfing tour in the 80s to finally win the World Title in 1993, but was not awarded prize money by the Association of Surfing Professionals. The patriarchal suffocation of women's surfing has trickled down to most line-ups. It has only been in the past twenty years that the slow acceptance of a variety of different boards for everyone to ride, as well as the growth of independent surfwear brands owned and run by women, has led to this sea change. The good news is surfing is the fastest growing sport for women in Australia. The once male-dominated line-up has slowly faded into history and now there is space for us.

I decided to start surfing in my mid-thirties. Being an adult beginner taking on the wild ocean is challenging and, at times, terrifying. Trying and regularly and spectacularly failing in front of strangers in a vast open space is also humiliating: there is nowhere to hide. For a paranoid beginner it was easy to read mockery in people's faces and think everyone was watching me. When I finally did catch a wave I asked friends on the beach if they had seen my triumph. Yet everyone had missed it. After this happened continually, I realised maybe no one was watching me after all. My embarrassment at my clumsiness faded and catching an unbroken wave seemed a real possibility. When I eventually did make it beyond the whitewash and joined the line-up, my fear of inadvertently getting in the way of another surfer left me with my heart pounding and nerves jangling. Yet even though my wave count was low, it was still so rewarding to see a surfer slide past with a smile enjoying their wave. Sometimes that was all the motivation I needed to summon the courage to paddle into the next one. Now I'm ten years in and have finally embraced my enthusiastic but average surfing. I implore anyone thinking about trying surfing to just have a go and feel the freedom, creative expression and connection to nature. Let's celebrate being average.

This book was born from a love of the ocean, surfing and our perpetual stoke on the people Willem and I have met on the waves or through friends of friends. We wanted to go beyond the perfect marketing and social media images of surfing and find out more about who surfers are. The women we have interviewed and photographed are strong, independent and community-minded. We talked to them about their relationship with surfing and the ocean, their passions beyond the break and the relationships they have forged in the community. This is certainly not a definitive book representing women in the line-up, and we are excited to see how surfing culture continues to open up to those it has excluded in the past.

Willem and I compiled these profiles during the pandemic, timing trips with impending border closures and lockdowns and road tripping thousands of kilometres. We made new connections and friendships over our shared passion and we thank every surfer who allowed us a glimpse into their surfing life.

Zoe

LIVES: HOBART/NIPALUNA
AGE STARTED SURFING: 7

DREAM SURF
BREAK: GREENS BEACH RIGHT HANDER
BOARD: 5'9" HAYDEN SHAPES THRUSTER
WAVE SIZE: HEAD HIGH

Marrawah is a tiny town on Peerapper Country in remote north-western Tasmania. Zoe's father inherited his parents' farm years ago and, with an eye on a right hand reef point, built a family home a short walk to the surf. Growing up, Zoe remembers the tight-knit surfing family having the break mostly to themselves, hooting each other into waves even in the depths of a southern winter. This sense of isolation has filtered into much of Zoe's life. She favours solitude over socialising, preferring to surf and paint alone. Through her paintings, Zoe is trying to unpack her visceral reaction to the landscape of home, stopping herself when she begins to romanticise the windswept hills and rugged coastline. 'I am forever trying to catch myself and wanting to remain quite raw and honest in the way I paint home. It actually can be really bloody difficult living there and really isolating.'

12

Surfing in winter requires tenacity and grit. 'There's nothing nice about it, it's just freezing cold, and your brain freezes and it's painful. And you get stiff. I've got Tassie blood, but I get cold really easily. In winter you can come out after a surf with your hair still dry and it doesn't feel super refreshing. You can feel like you've barely even touched the water because you just try to remove yourself from coming into contact with it wearing multiple layers of rubber. I say it's not very nice, but also surf as much as I can!'

As a teenager, Zoe began competing in board riders' events and soon became one of the top surfers in Tasmania in her age group. As Marrawah was so remote Zoe had to move away to complete her last two years of high school and for a while contemplated moving to the Gold Coast and engaging a surf coach to take her competing to the next level. Instead she chose to study locally and her quest to find people with who she could align landed her in the art department at her new school where she started to paint. Zoe is one of the rare art school graduates who immediately transitioned into being a self-funded, full-time artist with regular sell-out solo shows.

Zoe moved to Hobart a few years ago, but returns to Marrawah every summer to paint. She uses a shack right near the ocean and not too far from the family home as a makeshift studio. There's a space to paint, a couch, some beds and no running water in the bathroom. In between chasing waves with her brother or father Zoe will spend a few hours at the shack every day, sketching and painting. She'll then return to her Hobart studio to deep dive into painting, trying to make sense of the land she finds 'endlessly interesting'. She has a strong desire to connect to home and feel grounded, particularly when she's not there.

When Zoe surfs alone at the breaks around Marrawah, she's aware she is the only surfer in the water for miles yet she feels comfortable in the ocean. When she's out surfing, she's connecting to the place in a very special way. 'The way of viewing the land from the ocean disrupts the traditional sense of landscape painting. The perspective, when you're sitting on your board in the water, looking back at the land, is really unique.'

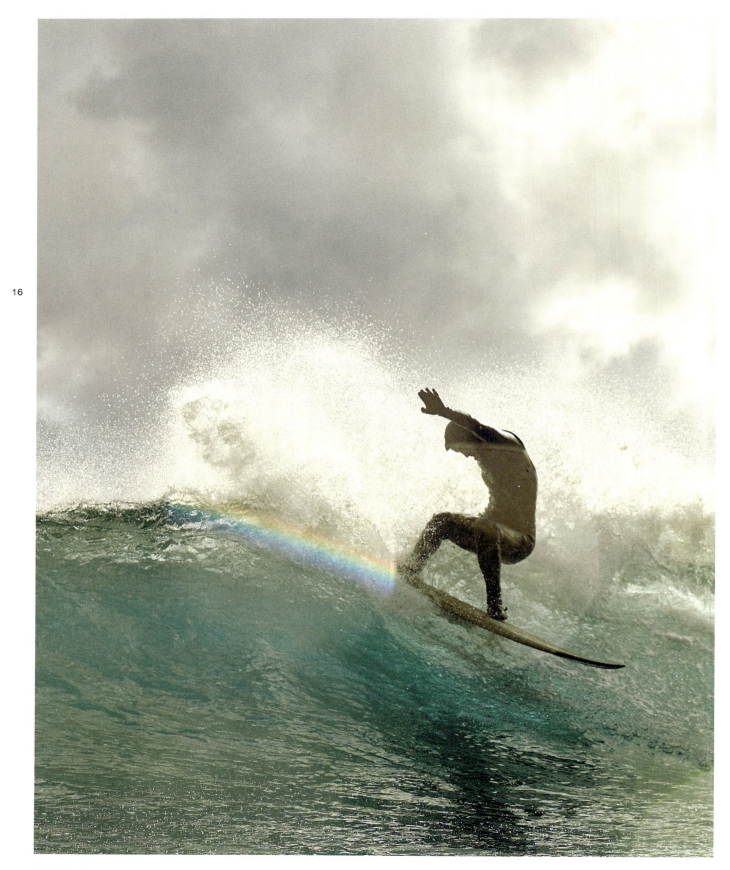

The perspective, when
you're sitting on your
board in the water,
looking back at the land,
is really unique.

ZOE

Lucy

LIVES: SYDNEY/GADIGAL COUNTRY
AGE STARTED SURFING: 14

DREAM SURF
BREAK: A RIGHT POINT IN MOZAMBIQUE
BOARD: 9'6" SINGLE FIN AND 5'9" TWIN FIN
WAVE SIZE: HEAD HIGH

Lucy never intended to be front page news. Yet her short acceptance speech while nursing a novelty-sized winner's cheque at the Curly Maljam quickly caught the attention of the media. 'Thank you to the sponsors for the money they've put into the event, but I would say it's a bittersweet victory knowing that our surfing is less than half of the men's prize money. It took the same amount to drive here, flights were the same cost and accommodation cost the same and our surfing is worth half as much. So maybe we can think about that for next time.' The story gained momentum and was widely covered in Australia and the UK, Germany and the US, and Lucy soon found herself doing interviews for television, magazines and podcasts. All the attention gave Lucy the impetus to push for a tangible change. She was a co-creator of the Equal Pay for Equal Play campaign, a campaign to change the way government funding is given to sporting clubs to ensure that there is equal prize money and access to facilities for everyone.

'When we use the argument of letting the market determine the amount of money that women should receive for doing sport, we're ignoring the fact that the market is sexist. So we need to intervene. We need to regulate what happens so that women receive their fair share.'

This has been an issue in surfing since women began competing over forty years ago and was recently documented in the *Girls Can't Surf* film. The documentary tells the story of a group of powerhouse female surfers in the 80s and 90s who worked within the unequal system, and constantly fought for a fair share of the prize money and the opportunity to surf in the same quality waves as the men. Before she competed in the local longboard competition Lucy had watched the movie and she felt it was time, yet again, to highlight the standard practice of women's prize money being less than half of the men's. 'I thought, this is more than thirty years later and it's exactly the same situation. Why isn't anyone saying anything?'

Lucy began competing as a teenager in her home town of Denmark in Western Australia. The general sentiment of the town was why would anyone want to leave when everything they needed was right there. But that didn't wash with Lucy. 'Any of the things that I'm doing now I could never have imagined for myself growing up because I didn't know that they existed.' Her first trip to South Sumatra to go surfing piqued her curiosity for new experiences, so her mother kindly bought her

a one-way ticket to Sydney. As soon as Lucy landed in Sydney she caught a train up to the Gold Coast and had her longboard sent over. Lucy landed a job at a smoothie shack and surfed her brains out, but the pull of learning was too strong and she moved to Torquay to study. Halfway through a degree in journalism, a close friend floated the idea of travelling to Africa and Lucy jumped at the chance. 'It was the most amazing trip and ended up being seven months with Anna and me egging each other on to be adventurous.'

This adventure kickstarted numerous travels and surfing experiences that have had an irrevocable impact on Lucy's life. Less than a year after she returned from the trip, the departure lounge beckoned and Lucy decided to study her anthropology and journalism majors remotely. She flew to Sri Lanka, then on to Madagascar and Mozambique. 'In Zanzibar, I got this idea that I wanted to go to the Middle East. So I just booked a flight to Egypt and I travelled overland into Israel and Palestine. I already had an understanding of how stereotypes form, how on the ground in these places it is always so different to the information we are fed. I met people who were just like me and had the exact same ambitions and the desire to have a normal life.' It was a watershed moment that shaped Lucy's understanding of the world. She returned to Mozambique for a few months, then headed to the UK and travelled through Europe and Morocco, returning home eleven months later via Vietnam.

These seminal experiences also shaped Lucy's observations of surfing culture. Once a surfer has made it in the line-up and has lost their beginner fears a new hesitation can creep in. Surfing is cool, right? But sometimes surfers can get caught up in the image – the beautiful board, the gorgeous swimwear – and not want to shatter the picture. 'I feel that's a huge barrier to progress. Many surfers in Byron try to cover up the fact that they can't really surf by crouching on their board. It's wonderful you're having fun, but really it is ego and not wanting to look like you're trying. I think it is way cooler to try and improve and hang five. The good surfers you're afraid of judging you are looking at you crouching and thinking, why aren't you trying?'

Lucy believes that surfing is an elite sport, not in performance but in a class way. She would like to see a concentrated effort made to make surfing a more diverse and inclusive environment. 'Just replacing men with women doesn't actually do anything. A lot of women do bring hostile attitudes into the line-up. It doesn't mean just because you're a woman it is suddenly so fun and awesome and wonderful; it's more complex than that. The line-ups in Byron are nicer because there are often more women, but increasing numbers is not the complete and only solution to changing the way hierarchies are established and managed in line-ups. Replacing men with women in any circumstance doesn't automatically mean there is transformation of the gender hierarchy.' Despite these deep complexities, Lucy enjoys sharing waves with women, especially the committed younger surfers. 'In my own experience, when there are a lot of girls out there, I'm less fearful of the hostile attitudes of the men. I feel really happy when there are girl grommets shredding. It's so exciting for the future of surfing.'

I thought, this is more than thirty years later and it's exactly the same situation. Why isn't anyone saying anything?

Angela

LIVES: TORQUAY/WADAWURRUNG COUNTRY
AGE STARTED SURFING: 2

DREAM SURF
BREAK: BROKEN HEAD
BOARD: 9'6" × 23" × 2 7/8" SOUTH COAST
WAVE SIZE: HIP HIGH

Angela's first memories of surfing are as a two-year-old, standing on the end of her father's longboard. Her parents were teenagers when they relocated to Byron Bay in the 70s from Sydney. Not long after they made a home in the still-sleepy town baby Angela was born. Angela's father is a keen surfer so when she was a toddler he popped floaties on her arms and paddled out to the mellow waves at The Pass. If Angela fell off after they caught a wave together, she'd happily bob around in the water until he would pull her up to paddle out again. When she grew older, Angela watched classic surf films on repeat with her father and little brother, like *Morning of the Earth* and *The Endless Summer*. 'There was a surfer called Rell Sun and she was always holding her own amongst the boys in these movies and I thought that was rad.'

As a teenager, Angela's father started taking her along to competitions and soon afterwards she was offered every surfing teenager's dream – a sponsorship deal. She was at her first-ever Noosa event and her father called her in and introduced her to Bob McTavish who said, 'Nice to meet you and welcome to the McTavish team'. Bob asked her if she would participate in a photo shoot starting in an hour. When she arrived at the photo shoot, bursting with excitement and nerves, it dawned on inexperienced Angela that 'I hadn't even shaved my legs'!

She was living the dream – paid to surf and travel the world with the McTavish and Ripcurl teams. After meeting Ian, her surfboard-shaper husband, Angela took time out from competing to raise her children, Charlie and Delilah. Any surfer who has a family wants their children to share the stoke of surfing and a love of the ocean. Angela believes you don't push your children into it. 'I just want to keep surfing in our lives; I want to keep it pure.' Angela shares waves with Charlie and Delilah, and during a recent surf with Charlie he asked her how he looked on a wave. 'I asked him what the main thing was about surfing and he said, "Paddling!". I said, "No!" and we went through a few more until he said, "Fun!" which was right.' For Angela the most important thing about surfing is to enjoy yourself and not stress about what you look like, who you're surfing with or who's who in the water. Just respect one another.

Angela and Ian co-own South Coast Surfboards, a thriving business selling hand-shaped boards to dedicated customers. 'Ian and I would never have crossed paths if I hadn't discovered longboarding – that's what I owe to surfing, meeting him.' Angela is always quick to smile and chat to anyone who may wander into their store and decide it's time to buy a board. She offers no judgement, only a charming grin and a readiness to share her surfing knowledge.

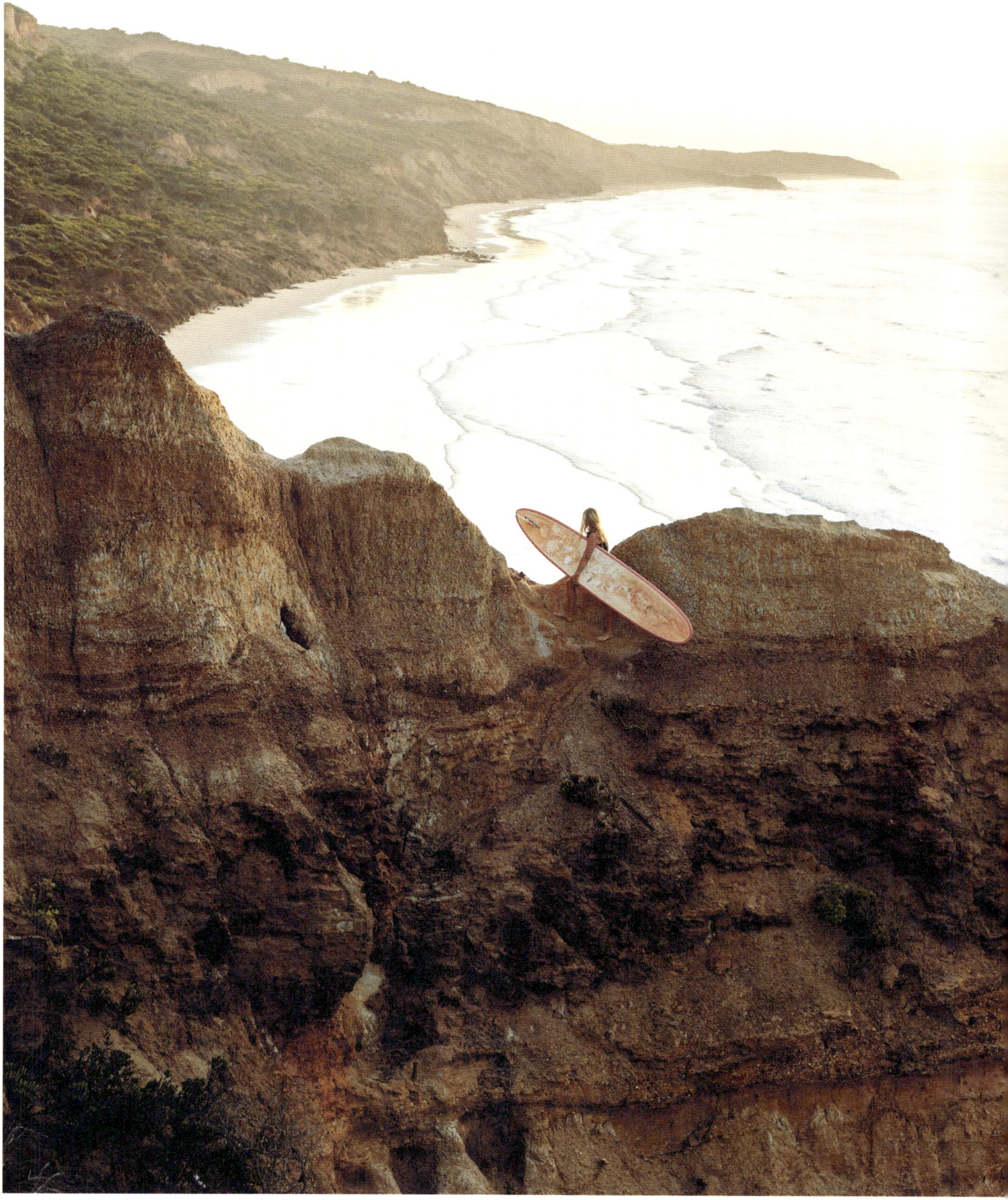

I just want to keep
surfing in our lives;
I want to keep it pure.

Zana

LIVES: BYRON BAY/BUNDJALUNG COUNTRY
AGE STARTED SURFING: 18

DREAM SURF
BREAK: POINT PLOMER
BOARD: SAM YOON MID-LENGTH
WAVE SIZE: SHOULDER HIGH

Zana has always felt a deep connection to the elements. She grew up roaming the bush with her siblings, riding horses and building cubbies on a property on the New England tablelands in New South Wales. Despite the ocean being many hours' drive away, as a young teenager Zana pored over the pages of *Chick* magazine, idealising and idolising the surfer girls. 'I always identified as a bit of a tomboy so I connected with these surfer girls, messing with the boys and contending with this wild ocean.'

When she was eighteen, Zana moved to Byron Bay and during an idyllic summer taught herself to surf. By the time she was in her mid-twenties she had fully embraced surfing and cemented a close friendship with another female surfer. When they weren't studying design and architecture, they would head south on road trips to Crescent Head where they would camp and surf for weeks. They were committed to their carefree life rather than 'feeling like we wanted to be in a relationship where we'd shape our life around guys. We wanted to be off on our own adventures'.

Zana now practises as an architect and continues to draw inspiration through surfing by being in the 'expansive wild nature, not looking back at the land, but looking out towards the ocean. I love being in my body and feeling the water on my skin. I love watching glistening shafts of light coming off the water, feeling the cool of the water and the warmth of the sun'. Those experiences carry through into Zana's creative practice because she's drawn to how she can manipulate form and material, and light and shadow and space to craft a sensory experience.

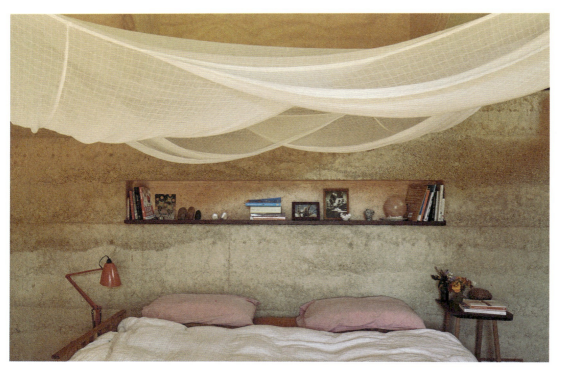

The off-the-grid home Zana designed and built is intended to be intergenerational – firstly for Zana and her young family, then for her parents when they are ready to downsize. The family live on a farm just outside Byron Bay's town centre. Zana's parents live in the original farmhouse and Zana lived in the old cow bales while she worked on the Quandong Cottage build. The surrounding landscape inspired the design in an immediate and functional way. 'The house is connected to its place by literally being made from it. A local farmer was clearing the stones from his property to make way for grazing, so we used his stones for our retaining walls. We built the earthen floor from clay dug from the site, combined with sand from the nearby Broken Head quarry, and sugarcane mulch from a local farm. The rammed earth walls are also built from earth sourced from a nearby quarry, and all timber in the house, including the ply, grew within a couple of hundred kilometres.'

The low-key home is nestled in a lush valley and feels spacious despite its modest footprint, due to the large windows and Zana's uncluttered style of living.

While regularly surfing at various breaks around Byron Bay, Zana has noticed that over the past fifteen years the increasing number of women surfing has changed the vibe in the line-up. She sees less of the aggressive,

macho mentality, which makes surfing more accessible for everybody. The warmer waters also offer an opportunity to surf in brief swimwear with titillating expanses of skin on view. This undoubtedly contributes to a sexual tension in the water that overflows into the carpark when getting changed, loose towels revealing flashes of curves. In one of the main surf carparks in Byron there are always clusters of vans parked and surfers loitering, standing by the gas stove to percolate a coffee, the exhibitionists among them wearing the minimal amount of clothing for as long as possible. Zana laughs, 'It's a place where people meet and you don't have many clothes on'.

Heidi

LIVES: NOOSA/KABI KABI COUNTRY
AGE STARTED SURFING: 6

DREAM SURF
BREAK: SAND BOTTOM POINT BREAK
BOARD: 9'5" THOMAS HIGH HEEL MODEL
WAVE SIZE: WAIST TO SHOULDER HIGH

Heidi feels she is a shy and awkward person yet when a board is beneath her she surfs with a graceful loose stance, intuitively walking to the nose as the wave rolls along. It's a surf style many beginners dream of but is usually the product of a lifetime spent in the ocean. Over the thirty years Heidi has been surfing, she has noticed a change from being the solitary girl in the line-up to, at times, the men being outnumbered. When she was younger she used to find it quite intimidating with so many guys in the water, yet overall Heidi's experience has never been particularly negative. She grew up surfing with Matt Cuddihy, Harrison Roach and Thomas Bexton and found them very respectful to the women they shared waves with. 'I don't know whether that was because they were just keen to see chicks in the water as there weren't as many of us surfing back then.'

Heidi tries to surf every day but finding the time as a parent when you have young kids is challenging, especially for a single mother. When Heidi has a day to herself she's up before sunrise and surfs until the moon comes up. 'I make the most of every second. The waves don't have to be perfect but I'll still be out there.' Sometimes while surfing a layer of mother's guilt can slightly dull the solo time, even if claiming a short half hour to surf is hard won. A few years ago Heidi separated from her partner and surfing kept her mentally afloat. 'Sometimes I would feel so guilty because I arranged for my kids to be picked up by my parents from school so I could go surfing. But I just needed to because mentally, if I didn't, I think I would have spiralled into a really bad case of depression. Surfing saved me during a really challenging time of my life.'

Like surfing, painting has always been a part of Heidi's life, with her seascapes often reflecting her inner world. In her early twenties she moved to Europe and would often surf in south-west France when she could escape the intensity of London and Paris life. When she was city-based, the feeling of displacement from the ocean translated into painting wave after wave from memory. This repetition of practice evolved into being a full-time artist, with her studio a short drive from her favourite point breaks. She finds that art allows her to escape into a creative and emotional place where she can digest her thoughts, and then release them. This is reflected in an intensity in Heidi's seascapes that sparks a curiosity to know what might lie beneath the churning waves.

Tia

LIVES: COFFS HARBOUR/GUMBAYNGGIRR COUNTRY
AGE STARTED SURFING: 6

DREAM SURF
BREAK: TEA TREE IN THE 1970s
BOARD: 9'6" SINGLE FIN
WAVE SIZE: SHOULDER TO HEAD HIGH

Tia's father, Rick, always hoped she would love surfing. They lived in a large hippie community on the mid-North Coast of New South Wales where Rick had painstakingly established a surfboard library in an old banana shed. The shed was filled with boards of all shapes and sizes and its sole purpose was to motivate a new surfer to borrow a board and give it a go. Rick had surfed his whole life and always encouraged Tia. 'I was very young when I first started surfing on the front of his board. He would take me to the beach balanced on the front of his bicycle, and we'd ride down and surf the boards that were stashed in the bush. I remember the day he finally talked me into going out on the board with him. I was looking at the ocean thinking it's too big and scary and he said, "Well, you either stay on the beach here by yourself, or you come out into the ocean with me". I tried to be brave and then I looked around and no one was on the beach so I got scared and called him in and he took me out into the surf with him.'

It brings me joy and
I can share it with my
father, children and
husband. It definitely
brings us together.

One of the deep pleasures of surfing is sharing the experience. Even if a fellow surfer didn't surf with you that day, they will revel in the stories of your waves. Tia can't imagine living without having surfing in her life. 'It brings me joy and I can share it with my father, children and husband. It definitely brings us together.' Tia, along with her husband, two daughters and her 'adopted surf daughter' Tamzen, regularly road trips interstate to compete. Tia had felt conflicted about entering competitions because everybody has a different style and preferences in how they like to surf. But after a period struggling with her mental health, entering the competitions gave her direction and meaning. 'It was really encouraging for my children to see me putting myself out there when I would never have done it before.'

Tia exudes a formidable strength and determination. It's hard to imagine her feeling rattled by other people's behaviour in the surf, yet it does happen. She is well versed in reading a line-up and is quick to judge the vibe, and will beach herself if she feels tension building. She recognises that it can take only one person to make the line-up feel busy. It doesn't have to be the number of people – just the energy. 'I surf for enjoyment and to fill a space in my soul. If I start getting angry or aggressive or feeling uncomfortable, I tend to go in. Sometimes if it's one individual and they're having a really hard time, I usually just give them space. I know it's not me, it's just a reflection of their consciousness and what's going on for them in their life at the time.' It could be that the surfer shuts others out by not making eye contact or responding to a friendly hello, or they could paddle around others to take a wave, or surf aggressively on mellow waves. Tia has the confidence to not be intimidated and the compassion to hope any lingering negativity will be washed away by the next wave.

Emma

LIVES: SURF COAST/WADUWARRUNG COUNTRY
AGE STARTED SURFING: 20

DREAM SURF
BREAK: AN UNPOPULATED ISLAND
  OF EMMA'S IMAGINATION
BOARD: 9'4" NETTLETON AND
  6'4" COREY GRAHAM SINGLE FIN
WAVE SIZE: SHOULDER HIGH TO OVERHEAD

Emma is a risk-taker. She surfed for the first time in the middle of winter in Norway, moved to Australia from Sweden by herself in her twenties and didn't just talk about 'living simply' but bought a yellow school bus with her partner to renovate and live in. Over three years they spent their weekends converting the bus into a tiny house while it was parked in the driveway of their share house.

When Emma was a teenager, her determination to leave her hometown of Umeå in Sweden and save money to travel landed her and her best friend Sanna a job in a fish factory in Norway – and an unlikely introduction to surfing. They had a weekend off from work in the middle of winter, so went to a local beach after renting massive foam boards. They dragged them through the snow to the water and then did snow angels to warm up. 'We were fighting the waves as you do when you try it for the first time, but I had so much fun.'

'The benefit of choosing to surf when you're an adult is that it's an active choice. You also remember the first time you stand up. If you're going to get anywhere with surfing, you have to be self-driven and really enjoy it because it takes so long to progress and you have to invest so many hours in the water.' Emma learned to surf for her own enjoyment and at her own pace, culminating years later when she could comfortably paddle out at Bells Beach on days where the waves are double overhead.

A few years after moving to Torquay, Emma met her soulmate Felix, a park ranger and fire fighter. Felix is a gentle man with a cheeky grin who loves surfing and adventure as much as Emma. They bought the school bus as a way to avoid being financially hamstrung by a hefty mortgage and be free of the rental market. The level of craft work and considered design of the bus is incredible. They handmade the parquetry floor, keep themselves warm with a tiny wood heater in winter and have the

choice of an indoor shower or outdoor bath. The bus is now parked on a friend's 10-acre property with a dam, chickens and abundant vegetable garden, and only a short drive from world-class waves. The bus is a family home too with beautiful Hendrix, who will no doubt be as stoked, passionate, creative and loving as his parents. 'The only disadvantage of being in a bus with a toddler is on really wet days and nights when you can see he's climbing the walls. I think it would be easier to live tiny when you're somewhere a bit warmer. Sometimes it would be nice to have space from each other too. The outdoor bath has been my room to go if I really need to do something for myself.' One day Emma and Felix might buy their own piece of land and live in the bus while they build a bigger tiny home. Meanwhile living in the bus enables them to save money, as well as travel for months overseas or on surf trips along the East Coast. Tiny home living really suits them.

they launched U&I, functional surfwear for ocean dwellers that is produced by local women. Their business grew beyond producing practical and stylish swimwear for active females to hosting events bringing like-minded women together. These happenings can be a morning learning how to free dive, or a surf meet-up for city folk and coast locals to swap tips and spark new friendships. The label has now expanded to include the Sunshine Coast, as Emma's new creative partner, Jen, is based in Noosa. Together they are dreaming up sustainable apparel for the surfing woman with a connection to the sea, who is interested in social change and supporting a small business.

U&I also co-hosts the annual Wild Women On Water event with the Surfcoast Longboarders Club. The event brings together women who enjoy healthy competition, whether they are first-timers or seasoned club competitors. The Wild Women participants say the bonus of the friendly event is surfing their favourite breaks with only a handful of other surfers in the line-up, a sentiment often echoed by World Surf League pro-surfers in post-heat interviews. Emma warmly welcomes all abilities of surfers in the line-up and is sympathetic to a frustrated beginner who wishes they were better.

About nine years ago, Emma moved to Torquay from Melbourne to pursue her dream of surfing every day, even through winter and the Southern Ocean's icy waters. Ever the problem-solver, Emma's idea of having a boiled kettle ready to warm her wetsuit before a surf is genius and takes the edge off getting changed in the Bells Beach carpark on a winter's morning when the temperature is close to zero.

Soon after Emma settled into living on the Surf Coast she met Jodie, who became her housemate and business partner. Together

The bus is now parked on a friend's 10-acre property with a dam, chickens and abundant vegetable garden, and only a short drive from world-class waves.

Jessi

LIVES: OCEAN GROVE/WADAWURRUNG COUNTRY
AGE STARTED SURFING: 5

DREAM SURF
BREAK: CRESCENT HEAD
BOARD: 9'4" PALE HORSE SINGLE FIN
WAVE SIZE: HEAD HIGH

Over the past ten years Jessi has been exploring her family's history. After discovering her Wiradjuri ancestry she was overcome with a grounded feeling. 'There was a generation of my family that were able to pass as white so they were able to leave the mission and move to Sydney to find work. So basically if they could deny being Aboriginal, they could get a job. My family didn't identify as being Aboriginal, but my nan knew so she passed it on to my aunty and my mum. My Aunty Lisa has picked it back up, and is trying to put all the pieces back together from what was lost through that period of time. It's been a slow journey, but one thing that I've learned is that it is already part of who I am, it's part of my spirit.'

Part of Jessi's journey as a Wiradjuri woman will be returning to Country at some stage, when the timing feels right. She has travelled across her ancestral land while heading north on many surf road trips but has yet to stop and connect. She's slowly preparing to take a trip out to Country and spend time there. Probably even take canvases and paint. Jessi's Aunty Lisa is an artist and when she was young Jessi would ask her to paint something for her. Aunty Lisa's response was to push Jessi gently to take up painting herself. It took a few years but Jessi eventually started to paint. The motivation to pick up the paintbrushes came when she was working in residential care with high risk youth. When Jessi started working there, she was exposed to a lot of violence and trauma. So art became an outlet for her. She tries to paint based on what she's feeling in her life at the time and to use Wiradjuri language to speak about it. Jessi

has been learning to speak Wiradjuri and the immersion in her painting style and connection to Country has led her to title her paintings in that language. She paints most days, creating commissions or works for herself. 'I think there was a part of me that was scared to do it, because I think I knew that it would almost unravel parts of me I wasn't ready to unravel.'

Since birth Jessi has always been deeply connected to the Birpai Country where she grew up on a farm in Bonny Hills on the mid-North Coast, New South Wales. Her father was a keen surfer so she and her sister were either in the ocean or at home making jumps to fly their bikes into the dam. Her love of where she grew up prompted her to find out more about the Indigenous history of the area. 'There's a headland you can walk up that looks over one of the beaches called Sharky's Beach. From there you can see Dooragan Mountain,

which is also called Big Brother Mountain, which is part of the Dreaming of Birpai. I love walking out there. But when it was colonised, they massacred all the Birpai people from that area, off the cliff there. It's called Grants Headland and the beach below is called Grants Beach, but we call it Sharky's because at the bottom there's grey nurse shark breeding grounds. When they massacred the Aboriginal people off the headland, there was a food source for the sharks. But no one knows the story. We don't get taught that stuff growing up because no one wants to talk about it. Whenever I walk up there, I can feel the spirits in those black cockatoos that live up there; I got this tattoo because it reminds me of the area I feel connected to.'

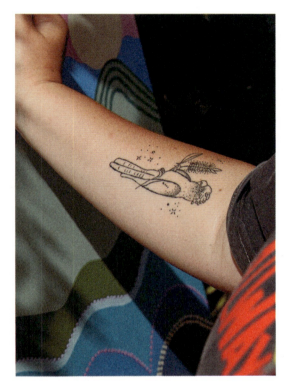

Jessi's warm nature and her love of connection and community feeds into her observations of surfing. She believes there needs to be a lot more compassion for people who are learning because everyone was learning at one point. 'We've all had really kooky moments where we've done something stupid. I surf with a bunch of women of all levels and when we're out in the line-up, it's fun. There's a heap of fun energy, even if it's the shittiest waves, everyone's having a good time.' Jessi feels sorry for a lot of the guys who are learning to surf because she doesn't think they have the same opportunity to just enjoy themselves. How refreshing would it be to see a group of male beginners in the line-up laughing and goofing around? Jessi's advice to any beginner surfer is not to challenge yourself too early and to stay in your comfort zone. 'You don't have to prove yourself to anyone. Don't feel you have to go big, or go home. I think the two most important things about surfing are having fun and being safe. Enjoy being in nature. You're connected to something way bigger than yourself that you will never probably fully understand. But that's the beauty of it.'

Lizzie

LIVES: BRUNY ISLAND/LUNAWANNA-ALLONAH COUNTRY
AGE STARTED SURFING: 6

DREAM SURF
BREAK: NIAS
BOARD: 6'6" GEOFF MCCOY
WAVE SIZE: DOUBLE OVERHEAD

Lizzie is one of only a handful of women who have surfed Shipsterns Bluff; a big-wave surf spot discovered only twenty years ago. It requires a two-hour hike through remote bushland carrying surfboards and gear before arriving at the base of a massive cliff, with a heaving wave exploding onto a razor sharp reef and tangles of kelp. The dangerous waves that can be up to 30 feet high are for only the most advanced surfers with steely nerves. When tackling waves with this much force and power, many surfers are towed into the wave by a jet ski. Only a small group of surfers have the strength and understanding to paddle into them. Lizzie decided she was going to paddle when she was just eighteen, the youngest surfer and only woman who has done so to date.

'Someone told me there was a swell coming and asked if I wanted to jump on a boat and come down and check it out because I'd never been there before. So I brought my stuff just in case and jumped in the water to cool off, but ended up surfing. I paddled for the whole morning and got absolutely flogged, getting wipe out after wipe out. I kept popping up and not feeling worried or stressed, just full of adrenaline and thinking, "Oh my god! Let's go again!"'

When the finicky wave is working it draws a small crowd of surfers, photographers and supporters. Lizzie regularly joins the line-up in the freezing cold water, alongside well-known big-wave surfers ready to tackle the wave for hours at a time.

Preparing to surf a huge wave requires a commitment to ongoing physical and mental preparation long before the actual day of surfing. In 2021, Lizzie was one of four women invited to join the Red Bull Cape Fear big-wave competition; the first time the competition opened the invitation to female surfers since it began in 2014. The group of twenty-four surfers are on stand-by from March to August waiting for perfect conditions and are given a day's notice to travel to Shipstern's Bluff. 'I think if I was really stressing out about the surf the night before, then I shouldn't do it. Usually I just get excited and really hyped up when I'm walking in and feel pretty level-headed because I tell myself it's just going for another surf.'

In recent times Bruny Island has become an enclave for the wealthy who love seclusion, architecturally designed homes, fine wine and cheese. Lizzie's family tapped into the quiet life long before living sustainably became a trend. Her parents bought an old farmhouse in the 90s to renovate and raise a family. Lizzie is well aware she hit the jackpot and is so grateful to have grown up there. It's not crowded and she can go surfing or fishing, have her own vegetable garden and chickens and live sustainably. 'Growing up here has made me realise what I want to do with the rest of my life — this is as good as it gets really. So that's why Mum and Dad haven't been able to get rid of me; I'm twenty-three and still living at home!'

A few years was spent chasing a dream to be a professional surfer, going on the qualifying tour with the expenses mostly self-funded from waitressing jobs at home. Lizzie worked long hours to save enough to travel to competitions but eventually realised chasing the competitions around the world was taking her away from a simple life on a small island off an island. She discovered that her island life could work in her favour and transformed her hobby of diving for abalone into a business.

Luna Collections sells jewellery carved from abalone shells in a tiny studio on the property. The business allows Lizzie the flexibility to chase swells when they appear as red blobs on a synoptic weather chart. 'I've always loved big waves. I like how they make me feel. I like how they've got power. As soon as you catch a good wave and get a good barrel, or if it's a bit bigger and you have a good take-off, you just feel a huge rush.'

Lauren

LIVES: BYRON BAY/BUNDJALUNG COUNTRY
AGE STARTED SURFING: 14

DREAM SURF
BREAK: ANY SAND-BOTTOM POINT BREAK
BOARD: 7'0" BING OMEGA MID-LENGTH
WAVE SIZE: OVERHEAD

Lauren was lured to try surfing as a young teen by a dream. 'I had a really vivid dream about surfing. When I woke up that morning, I felt like I needed to learn to surf that very day, so I had a friend push me into waves and from there I was hooked. I was lucky that where I grew up I was able to walk to the beach from home, not because we were rich, but it was in the 90s and living in a small seaside town was affordable. My mum was a single mum so I had lots of alone time because she was working so much; I just feel really grateful to have had surfing to keep me out of trouble.'

It wasn't long before Lauren began to enter the local surfing contests in Florida, more for the community spirit than the competition itself. When you're young surfing contests are just a day at the beach playing in the ocean with your friends and family. Lauren was part of a community of other women who were surfing at that time – Leah Dawson, Kristy Murphy and Jenni Flanigan. 'We lived in different parts of Florida and would meet up and share beautiful days outside together.'

In 2002, *Blue Crush* – a surf movie aimed squarely at young teens – was released and a surge of girls wanting to be part of surf culture soon followed. After women's competitive surfing had been ignored for decades, it was the profit-seeking surf companies that began to push women's surf to the front to capitalise on the zeitgeist. It was a really good time for Lauren to be surfing competitively because there was a big injection of support from the surf industry. Companies had finally realised that they could make money from women's apparel. Suddenly there were all-women's surf contests with a budget to offer prize money.

Surfing history is peppered with stories where a promising young surfer is faced with a momentous decision to chase waves with the financial aid of a sponsor, self-fund travel

to competitions with the hope that some wins will attract a sponsorship deal, or live a conventional life. It is an incredibly difficult decision to make, particularly for women who have a patriarchal expiry date due to their age. Lauren was offered an around-the-world trip with a sponsor but it would have meant leaving high school early. She decided to finish school and go to university to study environmental science. 'I had a pull to come to Australia so created a study abroad program at my university. I ended up at Lismore University, which is about forty-five minutes from Byron Bay. When I wasn't at class I would catch the bus into Byron, walk from the bus station to The Pass with my longboard and surf.' She met Dave, her partner and father of her son, Minoa, during that time.

a vegetable garden big enough to feed them and five other families. 'The idea was to have a surfers' garden that's resilient enough to be able to withstand weeks of neglect. When the surf pumps you want to be able to hit the road. I'm studying for my permaculture design certificate and I'm really inspired by the three founding principles of permaculture: people care, health care and the return of surplus. I think we would do so well as a surf culture to start having conversations amongst our local communities about what our guiding ethics are, what our guiding principles are, and really weaving that into surf clubs and boardriders' clubs.'

Lauren is one of only a handful of women who has carved out a space for writing in the surfing mainstream media. The rise of popularity of women's surf has created an opportunity for more voices to be heard through social media, crowd-funded magazines and podcasts. Lauren's latest project has been the *Water People* podcast she co-created with Dave. 'The podcast came about just after I'd had a very dangerous and traumatic pregnancy. I was sitting for many hours a day breastfeeding, as you do if you're lucky enough to get to breastfeed, and I just found my brain still wanting to engage. I didn't feel like I had the time to focus and write longform pieces in a way that I had done before. So the idea of a podcast came up as a way to still be able to engage with storytelling and connect with others in some way. In surfing, we often don't take the time to think about the whys of our surfing lives, especially in surf culture. We often think about the hows, how things are done, how to get here and there, and how to travel, but these surfing lives gift us so much depth and meaning and connection to ourselves, our community and the planet.'

Lauren left Lismore and went back to Florida to finish her degree, graduating just as the global financial crisis happened. She couldn't find a job in environmental science and was doing menial work to try to pay off her student loans while travelling and surfing. Then she got an email from Dave, who told her he'd bought some land and to come and visit. Lauren returned to Australia in 2010 and has been living here ever since.

Before Lauren and Dave started a family, they lived in an off-the-grid hut for three years – with no hot water or electricity – and tended a small vegetable garden. 'It was beautiful and romantic and challenging and cold when you got home from a surf and just wanted to have a hot shower.' Now they live in a recycled sustainable home and, with the help of a permaculture expert, have created

The idea was to have a surfers' garden that's resilient enough to be able to withstand weeks of neglect.

Gill

LIVES: KINGSCLIFF/BUNDJALUNG COUNTRY
AGE STARTED SURFING: 10

DREAM SURF
BREAK: KIRRA
BOARD: 9'2" THE GREEN PICKLE, SHAPED BY GILL
WAVE SIZE: SHOULDER TO HEAD HIGH

It was inevitable Gill was going to become a surfer. Her older brother and his friends would run through the backyard of their family home down to the break. Sometimes they would phone first and ask six-year-old Gill to look out the window for a surf report. 'I was pretty bad at it. They would come back from the surf and say, "What are you talking about? It was pumping!"'

When Gill was about ten she started badgering her older brother to give her one of his old boards. One day she came home and there was an old six foot brown board lying on her bedroom floor. Her brother made her give him $10 from her paper-run money. Gill now had oceanic freedom; it was time to teach herself to surf.

After surfing for a couple of years her hard-won confidence unravelled when a friend's board flew into her face, resulting in a serious injury and many stitches. Her friend was just learning, stood up in the shallows and shouted to Gill to look. Gill turned around, and the friend fell off the board and it went smack into Gill's face. 'I got back in the water after a couple of months but I don't think I realised until I was older that the accident had made an impact. There is an edge you need in shortboard surfing and that was gone. The accident really put me off surfing.'

Surfing didn't come back into Gill's life until she was in her thirties. Even though she had years of experience, her extended break from the water while she travelled and raised her children led to the wise decision to re-enter the surf under the guidance of an instructor. After a few lessons she realised her injury in the surf as a young girl had left her riddled with anxiety whenever she paddled out into a busy line-up. As she

surfed the popular world-class breaks around Coolangatta, she tackled her fear with the help of her coach and a beginner's foam board. Her confidence grew and her fear slowly diminished.

Gill returned to shortboarding but after a couple of years a ding on her board gave her an excuse to buy another surfboard. Surfers often look for any excuse to buy themselves a new board; the search for the perfect board can be as addictive as surfing itself. Unfortunately, when Gill visited a local surf shop, she was advised to buy a board that was totally inappropriate for the conditions she was looking to surf in. Feeling frustrated with her unsuitable purchase, she began researching the dynamics of surfboards and discovered a surfboard-shaping workshop with Richard Harvey from Harvey Surf. Gill signed up and was soon introduced to the minutiae of hand shaping. 'Before the workshop I thought there was thickness, length and colour in a board – and colour was the most important!'

Gill learned about the dynamics of how boards work, how water moves across the board, the three stages of rocker and how you have to match the surfer to the board and to the wave. 'Shaping my first board was like opening the door a crack. After finishing that board and going back to shape the second one, the door swung open. Now I'm on an endless hunt for the perfect board. If I make tweaks then I can't wait to get it in the surf to see if what I shaped actually works.'

Surfboard shaping is simply an extension of Gill's practice as a painter and ceramicist. She is an artist who works at both ends of the spectrum, from abstract to realism. It means constantly bouncing between exact details and an intuitive feeling with the hand, eye and touch, just as she works with ceramics. Gill exudes calm as she works in the shaping bay. Every movement is confident and considered as the blank piece of foam slowly transforms beneath her hands.

Surfboard shaping is a craft shrouded in mystique. Shapers work in backyard sheds or in shared bays in industrial areas. It takes hours of commitment under the tutelage of a seasoned shaper willing to share their knowledge, and surfboard shaping courses are a rarity. However, if a surfer is keen and

willing to learn, it doesn't take too much digging to find a mentor. Gill has shared her learning experience through her Shaped By She blog and Instagram, enabling a window into the intense learning process. It won't be long before she begins to take orders for her own hand-shaped boards and there are already keen surfers jumping onto her waiting list. Gill is aware of a move away from mass production, with surfboard hand-shaping following on from the handmade movement. People want things to last and get a board they can have for twenty years, rather than a mass-produced one that is replaced every year. 'I'd like to see more female shapers get into the game, whether they're hand-shaping or working on designs. As there are so many women entering the water now, it will just be a matter of time before there's a flow-on effect and we see movement into other areas of surfing. I started shaping as an average, middle-aged surfer. I have become a more advanced surfer through the journey of shaping.'

Sue

LIVES: NOOSA/KABI KABI COUNTRY
AGE STARTED SURFING: 58

DREAM SURF
BREAK: LITTLE COVE, TEA TREE, GRANITE
BOARD: 9'4" TOLHURST 2 + 1 SET-UP
WAVE SIZE: OVERHEAD

There is no other surfer like Sue. She decided to join the Noosa Heads Surf Life Saving Club in her fifties and soon learned to paddle a 5-metre surf ski and ride waves. 'I'm a Viking, it's in my DNA. When I go out and it's grey and there's the wind, the birds and the waves and my ski, I get this rhythm and I feel this power. I feel this is where I should be.' Seeing how at home Sue was in the ocean, her daughter Kristy suggested she teach Sue to surf at fifty-eight. She had just had a hip replacement, but drew on her strength from a lifetime of ballet and surfing came easily. She is as steady and sure within herself as she is on her board. In her experience of surfing, it's been all love and encouragement. 'I paddle out and say, "Is it friendly out here?" and smile. You can change the vibration when you paddle out.' In Sue's presence, her vibrations feel very high.

Once she started surfing, Sue took to it with such gusto that Kristy entered her into the State and National titles. In 2019, Sue became the Over 70s Australian Women's Longboarding Champion 'because there were no competitors for my age group', she laughs. She doesn't consider herself at all competitive. She joins in to prove to herself that she is strong, feeling healthy and can do it. Sue is an inspiration to many in Noosa and looks to women doing ballet in their nineties to keep herself motivated, believing if they can do it so can she. 'We all give each other hope.'

Coming to surfing later in life, Sue has an astute take on surf culture, particularly when there is tension in the line-up as everyone is aiming for a high wave count. 'People aren't fighting for the wave, they're fighting to be in the now. They are fighting to have the joy of being mindful. I don't think the people realise they're fighting to be in the present moment, when everything else disappears and the ego is no longer alive.' When Sue is out in the water she asks herself questions: Are you in the moment? Are you here? Are you experiencing this moment? Or are you just mindless? This striving to be in the now doesn't go unnoticed as some curious surfers have paddled over and asked her just how exactly she is having so much fun.

Sue's unique outlook has flowed on to Kristy who created the Surfdancer Academy of Surf in Noosa. When she was five she came across a photo from a newspaper of Sue doing a *grande jeté* on the beach and the caption read, 'Surfing by day, dancing by night'. Kristy decided she was going to be a surf dancer and dance on the beach and on the waves. She teaches students to express themselves through dance while surfing wearing costumes, encouraging creative movement. Sue believes 'surfing is a dance on the waves for everybody. The cutback, the looking, the lifting, it's a dance – the dance of life'.

Belinda

LIVES: AIREYS INLET/WADAWURRUNG COUNTRY
AGE STARTED SURFING: 14

DREAM SURF
BREAK: MACARONIS
BOARD: 6'4" NETTLETON EGG
WAVE SIZE: OVERHEAD

Belinda has been well loved and respected by many surfers for decades. Due to her outrageous talent she has been one of the lucky few paid to travel the world to surf in some of the most remote and wild places. After thousands of hours in the water, Belinda's passion to protect these precious ecosystems grew. She had been working with Patagonia for years and they appreciated her laser focus on activism, which evolved into her dream job as a Global Sports Activist. Having her son has driven her activism. 'I felt like I was always waiting for someone to speak up. But there were a few issues where I thought, No one is leading this one. Where's the research? Who's organising the beach clean-up? Then I realised that maybe I'm the one I've been waiting for. I'll die happy knowing that I've tried.' Belinda gives her time to other environmental organisations, whether it is working on the backend and helping with research, collecting data or fund-raising.

Belinda has started her own not-for-profit with some friends called Surfers for Climate, and is using her platform and voice as a surfer to try and prompt others to tackle environmental issues. 'It's my absolute dream job.'

Belinda's grassroots-driven activism hopes to encourage the surfing community to help protect the waves and environment. 'I would love to see all surfers in the line-up become protectors of our planet. We are so heavily reliant on a healthy ecosystem and so vulnerable to any climate impacts. A lot of those things get swept under the radar. It might be dirty run-off from bushfires that have occurred because of climate change. It might be coastal erosion because of erratic storms. It might be a rise in water temperature that has killed a bunch of seaweed or coral. The thing that we love so much is so vulnerable to any changes in an ecosystem. I really want to see all of us stand up and fight for what is right and hopefully prompt others to do the same. I'd love to see surfers become climate leaders.' There has been noted success with the Fight for the Bight protests that corralled surfers all over Australia to come together at local

breaks and paddle out in protest as well as sign petitions, which led to the environmentally dangerous exploratory drilling in South Australia being withdrawn. It is a relentless fight though: as one company withdraws, another announces plans to drill in other parts of the country. Drawing on her love for surfing and the community sustains Belinda's stamina.

better when they surf – a better take-off, turn, nose ride, cutback – and this can add a competitive edge, tension or frustration to the line-up. Perhaps a surfer keeps making the same mistake on every wave they have patiently waited for and paddles back out into the line-up muttering expletives of frustration. Or maybe someone has been surfing really well and starts to feel a bit cocky and drops in on someone who isn't as good but has travelled a few hours for their saltwater fix. If there's a woman who tries for a nose ride and wipes out with a shriek and paddles back out laughing, shaking her head, sometimes these tensions can dissolve.

Surfing has a spectrum of emotional, spiritual and physical experiences and its unpredictability feeds the addiction. 'It's playful, fun, healthy, challenging, scary. It teaches you the fundamentals of what builds a healthy strong character. There's days when it makes you feel like you're king of the world, then there's days when it makes you feel completely humbled.' Belinda loves the fact that there's a vast wilderness that's forever changing right on her doorstep, which can make her feel small and vulnerable and at other times empowered. In the end, surfing is about simplicity, being out in the ocean with a board and the waves. That's all she needs. 'It's great

Before Belinda became an activist, her rise to prominence in surfing was largely due to her being one of a handful of surfers who embraced single fin longboarding in the early 2000s when other styles of performance longboarding and shortboarding were dominating. Over the past twenty years, Belinda has welcomed the changes in the line-up as more women take up surfing. 'Women bring a different vibe in the line-up. There can be a lot more lightheartedness, a lot more fun, people shouldn't take themselves so seriously. It's okay to laugh when you fall! Surfing can be awkward and funny. Women bring a playful element to the water.' The majority of surfers are always striving to do

to share waves with people for inspiration and obviously to surf with friends, but you don't need any of it. You strip it all away and it's just about you, the ocean and riding the wave.'

An incomparable difference between men and women in surfing is the unexpected hurdles that may arise if you decide to surf when you're pregnant. What some of us don't expect is exactly how much this will impact on a surfing life. For some, surfing while pregnant is a goddess-like experience as they surf with strength, flow and creativity. Or the gentle bobbing of the ocean kickstarts nausea for the tenth time that day and lying down on a board makes their breasts ache. Belinda surfed until she was six months pregnant then stopped because it felt wrong. 'I was quite selective with the waves and where I went out. From about four months I just rode my longboard and surfed small waves by myself because I could control myself and my own board but couldn't control other people. I was

very hesitant surfing near people. I had a lot of people telling me to stop but I knew I'd stop when I needed to. I still swam every day. I'd like to say body surf but it was more like whaling around.' Up until the day before her son was born Belinda was still swimming in the ocean every day. She felt she needed to be in the sea. She had a lot of morning sickness – actually all-day sickness – and being in the ocean made her feel better. 'I hated the way my body felt. My back ached and felt horrible, so being in the ocean made my body feel normal again. That's why I just kept swimming and kept the connection with the sea and my sanity.'

Beth

LIVES: BONVILLE/GUMBAYNGGIRR COUNTRY
AGE STARTED SURFING: 20

DREAM SURF
BREAK: LOCAL SECRET SPOT
BOARD: 7'10" GATO HEROI SPACE PIG
WAVE SIZE: HEAD HIGH

It is not surprising Beth has attracted a community of surfers who congregate at her surfboard shop, The Water Closet. She is warm, quick to laugh, loves a chat and loves surfboards. Sadly, not long after acquiring her first longboard a few years ago she snapped it in the surf and was devastated. She searched to find someone to repair the damage and met Dennis Anderson, a local shaper. Noting her interest in boards, Dennis invited her to join him and learn the craft as he repaired and shaped boards. When another shed a few doors down became available for rent Dennis mentioned to Beth that if he was younger he'd open a surf shop. The idea resonated so she took the lease and opened The Water Closet's doors in Toormina on the mid-North Coast of New South Wales in 2016.

Being an avid op shopper and collector her whole life, Beth enjoyed road tripping up and down the coast buying boards to bring back to the shop. Word has spread about her knowledge and passion so surfers come to Beth to sell or exchange their boards.

Her honed collector's eye is drawn to single fin boards of any size and shape with her own quiver of around thirty boards constantly evolving. 'They're all so different. It's hard to let go of any as I tend to get a little bit attached to them.'

Before she discovered her love of longboarding, a friend taught Beth to surf a shortboard at a beach break. She struggled on knowing that even though she loved the ocean, her heart wasn't in it. A few years later Beth decided it was time to fulfil her dream of buying a longboard and she never looked back. 'Everything in my life fell into place after; it was so beautiful. I got a caravan, I found a vintage guitar and my first longboard.' Life is sweet on the mid-North Coast. Road trippers stop by to join the line-ups that swell and shrink with the seasonal holidays and if you

know where to look there is a treasure trove of vintage finds ready to be snapped up. Beth lives on an old banana farm her parents bought twenty years ago. She found herself the optimal spot in one of the paddocks and built herself a safari tent to live in with a view over rolling hills to the small surf town of Sawtell on the Central Coast.

As long as The Water Closet's doors are open, Beth will be there to listen to surfers' tales. She has found that everyone has a story to tell and they're all on a different journey. 'The surfing community is bonded by the love of the ocean and a respect for the environment and most try to do the right thing. There are also many people who want to go back to the old ways of doing things and this is reflected in their surfing. You can go out to a break and see a shortboard, a twin fin, a single fin, a bodyboarder, a surf mat, and a longboarder. I think that's cool that there are so many parts of surfing history all out there at the same time. It took us a while to accept each other, but we're all together now.'

Jess

LIVES: BROKEN HEAD/BUNDJALUNG COUNTRY
AGE STARTED SURFING: 15

DREAM SURF
BREAK: WINKIPOP
BOARD: 6'8" 70s HOT BUTTERED SINGLE FIN,
  SHAPED BY FRANK WILLIAMS
WAVE SIZE: OVERHEAD

A few years ago Jess headed north from her hometown on the Surf Coast in Wadawurrung Country in Victoria to surf warmer waters. She landed at a cabin her uncle had owned for years in a tiny pocket of paradise called Broken Head just before low-cost living in Byron Bay vanished. This affordable lifestyle allowed Jess to dive into her art practice far more deeply and quickly than if she'd been living in the city. Now she is able to spend long days in the studio in between her freelance design projects.

The idea of weaving with marine debris developed while Jess was on a surf trip to Mexico in 2008. She noticed the lack of waste management in the towns and cities she visited, yet naively didn't feel she contributed to the problem. 'As a traveller, you can easily extract yourself and think, "It's not my rubbish."' From Mexico Jess flew to New York and arrived in Manhattan pre-dawn where she had a life-changing realisation. She watched giant garbage trucks that looked like big, black beetles creeping across the street. She saw the piles of rubbish from the copious amounts of stuff consumed dumped on the sidewalk. 'It struck me that the Western world isn't doing a better job with waste, we're actually doing a far worse job, but we're just really good at hiding it from view. That was the moment when I assumed responsibility for the rubbish as well.'

When she returned to the Surf Coast she started noticing the increasing amounts of micro-plastic and synthetic debris on the shoreline. Motivated by her efforts to take responsibility, Jess began to collect polystyrene and work it into sculptures. After she began collecting the polystyrene she began to collect pieces of rope on the beach to create works. To execute her ideas for larger scale sculptures, Jess realised she

was going to have to find a huge amount of rope debris and wondered how she could get her hands on a few hundred metres at the very least. She heard of a group in Tasmania called the South West Marine Debris Cleanup where every year a group of twenty to thirty volunteers lives on a boat for a week and collects marine debris on remote stretches of coastline. She managed to land a last minute spot on the boat, and after a week with the group she returned with 500 kilograms of stinking rope, which she carted home in the back of her surf van.

The pieces Jess creates in her studio take many hours to create. She laboriously pulls apart hundreds of metres of rope into one single thread before she begins weaving. During the initial process she wears a mask to protect her lungs from inhaling the microscopic pieces of rope fluff that float through the air. Once the rope is unravelled, Jess uses various weaving techniques to create the organic works that form, spending hundreds of hours on a larger work. She likes to keep the pieces single origin, meaning the rope she finds on a beach creates a singular object. Her focus is on the material and the texture. She believes that if she plays too much with colour gradients, people won't notice the detail of the rope as much.

'Surfing has given me an appreciation and connection to nature and the natural environment. The connection between my art and surfing is noticing how we are impacting the world around us and creating a dialogue with my art. It's self-reflective and socially reflective of us as a society and what we value.'

Surfing has given
me an appreciation
and connection to
nature and the natural
environment.

Kate

LIVES: ANGLESEA/WADAWURRUNG COUNTRY
AGE STARTED SURFING: 18

DREAM SURF
BREAK: SECRET SPOT IN VANUATU
BOARD: 9'1" SOUTH COASTAR-18
WAVE SIZE: SHOULDER TO HEAD HIGH

Kate is a permanent fixture at many of the beaches near Anglesea. She and her dog greet the sunrise every morning at Point Roadknight then wander home for breakfast. Her carefully designed house is a surfer's dream, with a Japanese hot tub on the deck to soothe those sore muscles and a view looking to Point Addis where she can watch the weather roll in. Kate loves to cruise along the Great Ocean Road in her beautifully restored Kombi, or her shiny bronze Volkswagen Multivan, sometimes with her daughter Sam, sometimes solo, and with determined strokes soon be out in the line-up. Her presence can be intimidating. But like some other stern-looking surfers bobbing around in the ocean, this is usually due to poor eyesight and not her mood; although it would be advisable to remember your surf etiquette and not drop in on her wave.

Kate's surfing life has spanned over four decades and many styles of craft. She started kneeboarding when she was eighteen. 'Kneeboarding wasn't acceptable back then but I didn't care because it looked too hard to stand up!' She went on to windsurf for about fifteen years and then came back to kneeboarding. When Kate was thirty, her partner bought her a mal surfboard. Once she learned to stand up, her first thought was, 'I don't know why I didn't do this when I was eighteen!'

Kate and Sam have been surfing together for more than twenty years, travelling all over the world in search of waves. Kate taught a seven-year-old Sam to surf 'through much screaming and carrying on. I'd take her out to Cosy's or Roadknight and I'd push her onto

waves but she'd be yelling "No, don't push me off on that one! I don't want that one!" and she'd come in and throw the board down'. Years later Sam was surfing in the world longboarding titles and surfs with incredible intuition and style.

Parents who surf with their kids have a unique connection. Long drives in the car looking for waves can prompt a teenager into sharing stories that may otherwise be left untold. It's easier to talk in a cosy space with eyes on the road or the coastline than when sitting across from each other at the kitchen table. 'I love surfing with Sam and I admire her enormously; she's my surfing buddy. We'll jump in the old Kombi and go trundling down the coast. We've had some special surfs, just the two of us.'

Kate has seen many positive changes in surfing since she started, but feels there is more room for inclusivity and is working hard to make this happen. She joined Surfing Victoria as a Board Director and there is now equal representation of males and females on the Board. Surfing Victoria's role is to encourage people to be passionate about surfing and create pathways that promote diversity, with a focus on women and Indigenous surfers. Their regular Surf Her Way sessions coach small groups of women from Melbourne and the Surf Coast in improving style and refining skills. These sessions create a space for new friendships to bloom, the opportunity to gain confidence by surfing with other women and result in fostering friendly greetings in the line-up.

Kirra

LIVES: NOOSA/KABI KABI COUNTRY
AGE STARTED SURFING: 6

DREAM SURF
BREAK: CLOUDBREAK
BOARD: 5'9" RYPL BED WRESTLE MODEL
WAVE SIZE: OVERHEAD

Kirra has shaped her life around surfing. As a young teenager one of her first jobs was working at her local surf shop, Classic Malibu. The shaper, Peter White, recognised her endless curiosity and volunteered to be her mentor, teaching her the minutiae of the varieties of surf craft. Kirra was keen to extend her surfing knowledge into her tertiary education and completed a double degree in business and sports and exercise science. Her boundless enthusiasm has enabled her to compete on the world longboarding competition circuit while also running two businesses.

You can have the capability and the skills, but you have to have the confidence to own your place in the line-up as well.

Kirra works as a high performance surf coach for private clients and retreats with a focus on longboarding techniques. Her other business, Your Move Space, offers specific training in strength, mobility, cardio and agility for a variety of sports or fitness goals. 'I love seeing people progress. To see huge improvements just after a few sessions with a specific focus like cross-stepping, then continuing to advance to hanging ten and holding it in the pocket. It's great to share in their excitement.'

For a supposedly laidback leisure activity, there is a deep complexity to surfing. A surfer needs to know how to read waves, understand the weather conditions, be aware of surf etiquette – and actually surf. Plus you need hustle power in a busy line-up to claim a wave as yours. As the popularity of surfing increases, so do crowded line-ups, leading to frustration and disappointment. Layer on gender politics and it can feel overwhelming at times. Kirra has a respectful and dignified solution – develop your hustle power. 'You can have the capability and the skills, but you have to have the confidence to own your place in

the line-up as well. There is a level you reach in your surfing where you have to get in there and really go for it. I can see how it can be intimidating.' Kirra advises surfers to talk to people and be friendly in the line-up. They should pick where they are going to sit and not let people paddle around them. 'You've got to hold your ground a little bit. And if someone does drop in on you, politely call them out.'

When Kirra competes this hustle power also shines through. There is a strong contingent of Australian women who are good friends and travel together, and compete against each other on the World Surf League longboarding tour. 'It's funny, we travelled halfway across the world to Spain to compete in a heat together. In the water, you let your surfing do the talking, but if they make it through to the next heat and I don't, I would still be stoked for them as well. We've had the best adventures and it's so great to know when I get up at 6 am to look for a wave, they're right beside me.' It's the passion for sunrises, willingness to travel far and wide to find an uncrowded wave and long hours in transit that bind the friendships.

Jess

LIVES: BELLS BEACH/WADAWURRUNG COUNTRY
AGE STARTED SURFING: 26

DREAM SURF
BREAK: AN ISLAND IN INDONESIA
BOARD: LONGBOARD
WAVE SIZE: SHOULDER HIGH

Sometimes with surfing it feels like you can learn by osmosis. Surely if you watch your boyfriend surf for hours on end this will translate into also surfing with ease? Jess and Leo were madly in love on an east coast road trip when Jess decided to give surfing a go. 'I was very excited when I caught a wave and I looked around to see if Leo had seen it as I jumped off the board. The board kept going with my leg rope attached then flew up in the air and smashed me in the forehead with the fin centimetres from slicing my face in half.' Nursing a concussion and a huge lump on her forehead meant Jess took a break from surfing for a while. 'I was terrified.'

It's been a few years and now Jess is back in the water. 'My ego is not there as much as it was when I was younger. I'm not embarrassed to do things anymore and I'm not worried what people will think when I fall off my board, or what a wetsuit looks like on me. So I think the level of confidence that comes with age is really helpful to go out and try new things. What is really cool is the new challenge because surfing is not easy. Every sport has always been really easy for me so it's put me in my place. I like that because I just have to try harder and get better. I know I will.' She is really enjoying her time in the ocean, whether it is in the whitewash or out the back, and learning at her own pace.

Jess doesn't mind being a surf widow when the swell hits Bells Beach. 'You can't say anything bad about something that brings someone so much joy. It just makes me happy to see Leo come home beaming, dripping saltwater on the floor.' Jess and Leo struck rental gold with their 1970s architecturally designed house minutes from the beach. 'There's no insulation, so it's really cold but the shape of the house is just so weird and wonderful.' Jess spends much of her time outside on the 10-acre property using her machete and chainsaw, clearing old vegetation, growing plants in the greenhouse and sometimes crafting organic sculptures from small branches. As an interior designer, 'Leo likes everything to be precise and beautiful inside and I enjoy being outside, it's a happy juxtaposition as a couple. It's honestly a fairy tale house to live in'.

Daphne

LIVES: JAN JUC/WADAWURRUNG COUNTRY
AGE STARTED SURFING: 23

DREAM SURF
BREAK: SPARROWS
BOARD: 5'9" DHD TWIN FIN
WAVE SIZE: HEAD HIGH

Traditional Chinese medicine practitioners consider someone with bright eyes to have a strong shen, or life force. Daphne's eyes are always shining with enthusiasm, ready for the next adventure on the horizon. Daph spent her childhood in Ipoh, Malaysia. 'I grew up nowhere near waves yet somehow I've always been drawn to surfing.' She moved to Melbourne to study communication design in her early twenties and as a post-graduate scored her dream job working for Rip Curl and moved to Torquay, the home of the Australian surf industry since the 1960s.

Working for a surf company and living by the beach has its perks – you share a common passion with your workmates, and surfing during your lunch break is encouraged. Daphne taught herself to surf by embracing the culture and lifestyle, trying to surf up to three times a day and daring to push herself to go out in conditions above her skill level. During a big swell in Torquay, a surf carpark will be full on a weekday, with lunch hours cheekily extended and people returning to work with wet hair, salty skin and stories to exchange. Daph feels a lunchtime surf 'is a reset button – you start the day anew'.

Another perk is the occasional overseas surf/work trip. Years ago Daph was chosen as a part of a small team to go on a boat trip for research. The 'Tip to Tip' trip involved the team travelling by boat from one end of Indonesia to the other, stopping to surf along the way.

The part of the trip Daph joined was when the boat circumnavigated Lombok and Daph was lucky enough to have the best surf of her life, scoring perfect sunset waves at a remote spot she hopes to find again some day.

Daph has always been drawn to travel. Her Swiss mother and Malaysian father met in London and soon after her mother followed her love to Malaysia, where they married and raised four children. Daph met her British husband Oli in Mexico and, like her mother, he followed his heart and moved from Europe to live in Torquay. Daph and Oli match each other with their enthusiasm for travel and love of the outdoors. When he arrived in Torquay, Oli bought a Renault Master van and spent months fitting it out and turning it into a haven of comfort. There is a cosy couch, and a bed that feels like you're sleeping on a fluffy cloud, plus a kitchen, shower and toilet.

Caption

But is living in a van with your husband as romantic as it seems? 'We get along so well we never feel like we're in each other's space. We're a really good team.'

Oli is a quiet achiever. He has rockclimbed all the major peaks in Yosemite numerous times, became a master diver as a teen and has coached the New Zealand Olympic ski team. He took up surfing after he met Daph and it is tempting to wonder if there had been a power dynamic shift in their relationship since sharing waves together. After all, Daph has been surfing for over ten years and, as experienced as he is, Oli was still new to the line-up. Daph chuckled at the speculation. 'It's nice to have a different skill to Oli, and be a little bit bossy in the water, not that he listens ... But Oli knows I can read the ocean better than him.'

One of their more recent trips before the pandemic was finishing the ski coaching season in Austria, then climbing a 4000-metre peak in Chamonix – a mixed climb, including ice axing in the snow, rockclimbing and traversing some glaciers. 'I made him do the Tour de Mont Blanc hike. I have softened him and now he

doesn't do as much dangerous stuff.' Only days after we photographed Daph and Oli, they were flying to Bali to search for the perfect wave from Daph's Rip Curl trip, then they were off to hike to Everest Base Camp. Spending time with Daph and Oli makes you feel like any adventure is possible – just pack a bag and board and go. But, as Daph likes to say, 'surfing is the funnest'.

Kerry

LIVES: ANGLESEA/WADAWURRUNG COUNTRY
AGE STARTED SURFING: 24

DREAM SURF
BREAK: RIGHT POINT BREAK
BOARD: 9'1" GREG BROWN HIGH PERFORMANCE
WAVE SIZE: HEAD HIGH

Kerry is the surfing cheerleader everyone needs. Her own introduction to surfing was such a negative experience she gave it away for seven years and didn't take it up again until her early thirties. As a beginner she got in the way and was abused a few times. 'It crushed me. I was desperate to learn how to surf and my self-esteem took a massive hit.' Kerry didn't start surfing again until she had stopped caring about how good she was and what other people thought.

When Kerry moved to the Surf Coast and decided to re-enter the water she had a completely different experience. A lot of the older men in the community really welcomed and encouraged her. They gave her pointers when she asked for them and helped her learn how to read the weather charts and the swell. 'They could see the passion and how hard I was trying. They saw me around on my own a lot. I was just always sitting there smiling, ready to have a conversation.' There is something to be said for learning to surf on your own or with one other buddy. Sure it can feel like there's safety in numbers, but a large group of beginners paddling out can be met with eye rolls and disgruntled mumblings. It is a challenge to paddle out alone as a beginner. But with an open mind and a willingness to watch and ask questions it can speed up your learning process. You can also make some surfing friends who will watch out for you.

Kerry encourages other women who come out looking really nervous, trying to put them at ease just like the older surfers did for her. 'When someone's on a wave and they've never met me, but I'm cheering for them as they go past, you can see the stoke. It's awesome.'

Kerry is one of those surfers who loves to be the first in the carpark to watch the sunrise and the last to leave. In surfing parlance, a mad frother. She'll go out in any conditions. 'I will still go for a paddle if it's flat, it is a great opportunity to work on my paddle strength.' She'll even go out for one wave if she's short on time. Her love for surfing and her desire to encourage more women to join the line-up has evolved into surf coaching with Emma Webb at She Surfs Surf School. 'I'm a teacher and love teaching people new things. I love seeing people learn something.' Kerry and Emma have coupled their two favourite pastimes of art and surfing to host surf and craft weekends.

Kerry has always created. She draws, paints, collages and makes ceramics. Her felted artworks began as an experiment for a women's surf film screening in Torquay. Some local female artists were displaying surf-related work as a part of the event. Kerry tried some paintings and drawings, but felt they were quite average. When she found a supply of felt in her art supply box she started to experiment and couldn't believe it actually worked. 'I think the first one took maybe four hours to create and now pieces can take up to forty hours. While I do love the more complex and detailed artworks I'm now creating, part of me still wants to go back to that simplicity. I guess that's kind of like surfing. You can go out and get the fanciest board and all the gear, but at the end of the day you just want the simplicity of paddling out and catching a wave.'

A small group of women spend a weekend together crafting – it could be an artwork or making an alaia surfboard – in between surf-coaching sessions. 'We love connecting women who want to meet other women with similar interests and passions. We get women who have never met each other, spending three days together, learning a new craft or skill and receiving surf coaching, and making new friends.'

Poppy

LIVES: ELANORA/YUGAMBEH COUNTRY
AGE STARTED SURFING: 14

DREAM SURF
BREAK: TROPICAL REEF BREAKS
BOARD: 6'6" TAKEDA CUSTOM
   MODERN SINGLE WITH 2 + 1 SET-UP
WAVE SIZE: HEAD HIGH TO OVERHEAD

As she was growing up, Poppy and her family moved around a lot. They lived in Papua New Guinea, a remote Indigenous community in South Australia, and eventually settled on a farm on the Sunshine Coast in Queensland, where Poppy discovered her love for surfing. She went from living in an Aboriginal community to going to a surfy high school in Coolum. Inspired by her brother and his surfer friends, Poppy decided to learn how to surf on a shortboard −'the worst craft to learn how to surf on' − and struggled to stand up for over a year due to the board's small size. Despite the challenges she still loved surfing with her high school girlfriends.

Surfing fell off the radar when Poppy went to uni straight after high school, then decided to head to the mountains and snowboard. Poppy continued to travel throughout her twenties. She lived overseas in Asia working as an English teacher and then a fashion designer. When she returned to Australia she started working for Billabong and a return to surfing naturally followed.

This rediscovery of surfing was cemented when she married a surfboard shaper called Yoshi, who inspired and encouraged her. Poppy met Yoshi in between design jobs while she was managing a small surf shop in Currumbin. 'One of my favourite surfing memories is when we went on a surf trip to the Mentawis. I realised how much I loved surfing. Those waves were the most perfect waves to challenge myself on and improve. I just remember coming back with a different

level of skill. I wasn't afraid of bigger waves and I felt confident. It feels so good to go so fast doing nice big turns, that's my favourite wave.'

Before her Mentawis surf trip, Poppy struggled to find suitable swimwear she liked, so decided to sew herself a surf suit with long-sleeves to protect her skin from the tropical sun. She drew on her skills as a fashion designer honed over years working for surf and swimwear brands and realised her surf suit was a success. It looked great and stayed in place even when surfing in challenging conditions.

After she returned from her trip, TallPoppy swimwear was created. Poppy wanted to share her designs with other surfers who were tired of adjusting tops and wrestling with bottoms as they try to keep breasts and bums covered.

Every piece of swimwear is touched by Poppy's creative hands from start to finish. Poppy has stuck with full coverage, more to highlight her vintage-inspired textile designs rather than protect a surfer's modesty. She designs the styles and prints, creates the patterns and cuts, and sews every item of swimwear in her studio. 'I've always loved vintage and trawling through op shops; it has been my style ever since high school.' She started working with a supplier and found out she could print her own designs onto sustainable fabric made from recycled plastic. Poppy thought that was a great way for to go. 'It's in line with my ethos of slow fashion and making everything myself.'

Anna

DREAM SURF
BREAK: CROFTS
BOARD: 7'0" MODERN LOVE CHILD MID-LENGTH
WAVE SIZE: HEAD HIGH

There are people who enjoy hobbies and then there's Anna. She loves surfing, diving, motorbike riding, ceramics, cooking, gardening, shooting, oil painting and fishing. Many of these activities are enjoyed with her equally enthusiastic partner, Simon, on a 100-acre property only a ten-minute drive from the surf. They have been renting a 1950s farmhouse on the farm for the past few years, and with paddocks to ride their motorbikes on, shooting targets set up to fire their .22 shotgun at, and an abandoned wool shed turned ceramics studio, they have plans to stay for a little while longer. 'It's all about giving the activities a good crack and enjoying the freedom of working for ourselves from home.'

Anna only recently added ceramics to her list of interests and she's hooked. 'It's my calling. It's repetitive. It's perfectionism. It's working with my hands. It's creative. It's the freedom to think of something and then actually moulding it into clay to see if it worked.' All the activities are an unconscious strive to be in the moment and to have a good time. 'I like change and I like delving into something new and just learning.'

Clearly not shy of venturing off into the unknown, Anna decided to learn to surf by enrolling in a ten-day surf camp in Sri Lanka. She took to her first surfing safari with such fervour that she decided to travel to India the following year. However, the second trip proved to be somewhat hair-raising when she was run over by a fishing boat and nearly killed. Anna had been surfing a wave off a pier popular with fisherman and a small band of surfers when she had to ditch her board and dive to the shallow bottom as fast as she could as a massive timber boat and its propeller sped over the top of her. Needless to say her confidence was shaken. Since then she and Simon hunt for empty stretches of beach along the Great Ocean Road rather than being a regular at the popular local breaks.

'I try to not take it all so seriously and think I'm going to be an amazing surfer. I'm going to do it as a hobby and as something to do with friends. I can surf to the point where I can come out and paddle with you and have fun. What keeps bringing me back is the community and the social aspect of it – the feeling that comes after a surf. Even if you don't do it well, you've always just had the best day. Even if you've had a knock on the head, at least it's a good story.' Surf lore tells us the best surfer out in the line-up is the one having the most fun and Anna is one of those surfers. She is quite happy with her ability as an average surfer. This, coupled with her optimistic appreciation of the whole surfing experience, is a reminder to any surfer overcome with the sinking feeling of comparison that it's a sweet privilege to be on a board floating in the ocean, let alone finding the countless hours of water time needed to progress. Surfers, even the average ones, are pretty lucky people.

Ella

LIVES: TORQUAY/WADAWARRUNG COUNTRY
AGE STARTED SURFING: 8

DREAM SURF
BREAK: KENNETT RIVER
BOARD: 5'10" FINELINE FISH
WAVE SIZE: SHOULDER HIGH

Ella can clearly remember catching her first wave. She was at her home break in Apollo Bay catching waves on her bodyboard when she accidentally dropped in on an older surfer on a longboard. Before she knew it, she'd been lifted up by one arm and had joined him on his board and together they were surfing along the smooth face of the wave. Ella instinctively held her arms above her head with joy, her bodyboard still attached to her wrist flapping behind her. From that moment on, young Ella knew surfing was going to be part of her life.

After she had discovered surfing, Ella's father decided to always say 'yes' every time she asked to go to the beach. Unlike some parents, her surfing dad didn't take the super coach approach – the surfing equivalent of a stage mother – but gently gave her tips only when asked. The best advice that Ella remembers is 'any surf is a good surf'. Even if you fall off every wave or the wind is howling or the line-up is ridiculously crowded, a surf still leaves you feeling rejuvenated.

Every young surfer benefits from a *Point Break* Bodhi-like figure to look up to – a positive spiritual guide, surfing sensei, ocean guru, call them what you will. Ella's Bodhi was an older friend in her late forties who would pick Ella up at 6 am to go surfing and would drop her late to school. Back then there weren't many women sharing waves and Ella loves how many women are surfing now at many of the beaches she visits. Just like a surge in swell, Ella feels there is a momentum building among these women taking to the waves. Ella's ultimate goal is to simply keep surfing for as long as possible, until she's eighty at least. 'Of course I'd love to be catching stand-up barrels in remote tropical places but I'm happiest to be in the ocean, catching waves for as long as possible.'

One of Ella's most memorable surfs was when a friend convinced her to join him when no one else was out. The waves were over three times Ella's height when a huge ten foot set wave pummelled through the bay. Ella watched the wave rolling towards her, thinking, 'looks like I'll be held under for a really long time and I will probably wake up in hospital'. The wave tumbled and crashed over her and after being somersaulted in the deep for what felt like minutes she popped up gasping for breath.

She clambered back onto her board and looked over to her friend floating nearby, his board nowhere to be seen. He casually said, 'I think we should go in'. Despite this experience Ella's only fear of the ocean is one of pulling back from paddling into a wave. The experience of the hold down during that surf would rattle even the most experienced of surfers, yet it is the fear of lacking the confidence to tackle a steep drop of a wave rather than the ferocity of the ocean that spooks Ella. This is one brave lady.

Julia

LIVES: BONDI/GADIGAL COUNTRY
AGE STARTED SURFING: 10

DREAM SURF
BREAK: LEFT HAND REEF BREAK
BOARD: 9'1" TAKAYAMA STEPHEN SLATER MODEL
WAVE SIZE: SHOULDER TO HEAD HIGH

If you are a surfer with children, as soon as they are able to swim, you sit and wait – and hope – for the day they show an interest in surfing. 'My daughter's thirteen and my son's eleven. I think because I'm so desperate to go surfing all the time they look at me and roll their eyes. We do spend a lot of time at the beach and I will always take a whole lot of foamies plus their boogie boards just in the hope that they'll say, "Mum, can I take a board out today?" But I don't want to force it on them. I want them to love it.' Julia's enthusiasm for surfing and her son's curiosity led to a weekend trip to Melbourne at the Urbnsurf wave pool. Maybe the opportunity for fifteen waves in an hour will spark something and soon Tom will be surfing with Julia at home.

Julia's local break is Bondi, one of Australia's most famous beaches, and she has been surfing there for most of her life. Bondi is now so popular that one end of the beach has a foam boards only rule to avoid potential injuries and board damage. Julia channels serenity and patience, and employs a dash of sleuthing, when joining the line-up. Her eagle eye and flexible working hours give her the chance to jump in when she notices a lull in numbers. She doesn't like the feeling of competition or the fear of doing something wrong. There are so few waves at Bondi that if you mess up someone's wave you hear about it. Julia was once chased out of the water and up to the carpark by a guy after getting more waves than him because she was on a longboard. That experience has made her very cautious and aware of others. 'I try to bring a positive feeling out in the surf and make sure everyone gets their fair share.'

On days when the Bondi line-up is heaving with predominantly male surfers Julia and her friend mark it as a BD day – Big Dick Energy. Julia will then take a deep breath, paddle out and hope that her patience and awareness subtly change the dynamic. Unfortunately Julia knows that when you get into an environment where there are fewer waves and people are short of time, localism and tempers can flare.

Julia and her husband have been living in Bondi
since their twenties, renovating and selling
houses. One of their most recent projects –
Bismarck House – is a holiday rental house
tucked down a laneway and only a short walk
to the beach. They lived in it for eighteen
months during the first Covid lockdown. 'It was
a really cool space to live in. It is right in the
thick of it and it's just a roll down the hill to
Bondi or Tamarama. There is a timber window
seat that opens up to the laneway and that's
where I sat during lockdown while my kids
were homeschooling on the round dining table.
I had it pretty much open all lockdown and just
watched people go by. I think that's one of the
nice things about Bondi. There are so many
people and it's such a vibrant community.'

Stevey

LIVES: BYRON BAY/BUNDJALUNG COUNTRY
AGE STARTED SURFING: 9

DREAM SURF
BREAK: THE PASS
BOARD: 9'5" NETTLETON MULTIPLY
WAVE SIZE: OVERHEAD

Stevey is from a fourth generation Byron Bay family. However, the rapid change of the cultural fabric in her home town over the past few years has been bittersweet. 'I feel strongly connected to the place, even though it doesn't resemble the town I grew up in. Byron Bay people to me are surf bogans; blue collar, salt-of-the-earth people who look after each other. Now it feels there are too many opposing values of wealth and status versus sustainability and wellness competing against each other in a small town; Byron is just trying to be too many different types of things.' Stevey is in no rush to leave town though, where she has a very close relationship with her mother, Debby. They are quick to laugh and tease one another as they share stories of The Bay, which is the way the town is referred to by the true locals.

As a child, Stevey remembers spending every weekend from sun up until sun down at either Wategos or The Pass with Debby. Debby was the first female president of the Byron Bay Malibu Club in the late 90s and Stevey spent many weekends watching the competitions, learning to surf by total immersion. As a teenager, being one of the only girls in a small line-up was never an issue. She was a tomboy growing up and had very strong female role models like her mother. 'I was taught to stand up for myself and have always felt calm, comfortable and confident in the water.'

Despite living in a town in a state of cultural flux, Stevey realises that the natural beauty of Byron Bay isn't going to change — and the waves are still the same. Unlike a generation ago when you knew everyone in the line-up, now a point break is shared with up to a hundred other surfers who cover the full gamut of abilities. Stevey either has to channel patience and positivity before paddling out or head to a less crowded beach break for a quieter surf. Chasing the joy of catching a wave in crowded conditions is a challenge but feeling time collapse when surfing a wave is always worth it.

Despite mourning the changes of the town she grew up in, Stevey has decided to capitalise on the influx of newcomers by sharing her knowledge in the hope it will influence future surfers. She plans to start her own business, teaching people how to read the natural world and the surf conditions, and how to slow down and reconnect with nature.

Jude

LIVES: COOROY/KABI KABI COUNTRY
AGE STARTED SURFING: 19

DREAM SURF
BREAK: TEA TREE
BOARD: 9'3" HARRISON MODEL, THOMAS SURFBOARDS
WAVE SIZE: HIP TO SHOULDER HIGH

In many surf towns a true local is someone who has lived in the area for a couple of decades, minimum. Classify yourself as a local any time before that and you'll receive some raised eyebrows and indecipherable muttering from the older surfers watching and judging the local break each and every morning. As a Noosa resident for the past thirty years, Jude qualifies. Jude was taught to surf by her partner in her late teens and was quickly hooked. She still dreamily remembers catching her first green wave.

Parenting a brood of five children meant a ten-year hiatus from surfing for Jude, as she was otherwise occupied raising her family on a farm a short drive into the Glass House mountain range near Noosa. Now that her youngest children – twin boys – are teenagers, Jude can be found strolling down to Tea Tree as dawn breaks, longboard balanced on her head and wishing other surfers a good morning. 'On the walk to Tea Tree there's a spot where you walk through a grove of paperbark trees and it feels so quiet and peaceful. It makes me feel so calm.'

As Tea Tree is one of the most popular longboarding spots in Australia, serenity is a must. There are many different approaches to handling a busy break – the right attitude, knowing where to sit and, most importantly, being aware of the movement in the line-up. Jude navigates the busyness by constantly watching the other surfers. As the sets roll in, Jude will usually sit on the shoulder and slightly inside to everyone else, alert and waiting for an opportunity. A wave can crumble then reform, a surfer can fall off, or if Jude feels the need to police she will 'just drop in on someone if I think that they've been catching too many waves and I haven't'. This is a controversial method but her approach is rarely questioned, so her judgement must be considered fair by the other surfers.

Some people can grumble about their home breaks being too crowded but Jude radiates positivity and is always smiling as she surfs. 'It's not how well you surf in the line-up, it's your attitude. A line-up is a micro-community so when you paddle out with a smile and a good vibe, good things will happen.' Jude has embraced the crowds and feels that more women in the line-up has made it feel calmer, even with the extra hooting and shouts of encouragement she happily gives as a surfer slides past her having a great ride.

Rebecca

LIVES: BRISBANE/TURRBUL COUNTRY
AGE STARTED SURFING: 25

DREAM SURF
BREAK: MANU BAY
BOARD: 9'3" SINGLE FIN ASTRO BY GARY BURDEN
WAVE SIZE: SHOULDER HIGH

Over the past few years The Pass in Byron Bay has been well documented by many a social media account. Glorious sunsets with stylish longboarders balletically cross-stepping is standard fare. So for someone learning to surf perhaps it wouldn't be the ideal spot to be pushed into the waves by a friend. Learning to surf isn't exactly graceful. Sometimes there's snot streaked across your face, with arms and legs akimbo as you unceremoniously fall off yet another wave. 'It's so embarrassing learning to surf! I call surfing ego maintenance.' Bec is proud of the fact that she is resilient and has the kind of ego to persevere and keep trying.

After completing her degree in her mid-twenties, Bec was mooching around in her hometown of Byron Bay, making jewellery, working in a cafe and surfing, when a family friend told her that if she wasn't happy then she was wasting her life. Bec's observations of surfing culture had piqued her interest in research so she embarked on a PhD on women's surfing in Byron Bay. This blossomed into an ongoing academic career studying surfing, the ocean and the surrounding communities for over ten years. 'The best interviews for my PhD were when women wouldn't tell me how things should work. Instead they said do what you want. You can drop in on men if you want, wear a G-string if you want, sit on the outside if you want, but whatever you do, understand that it has effects on other women.'

There is only a small group of women who have been tackling the politics in the line-up, ongoing under-representation of women in surf culture and sexism in the surf industry. Bec has been writing about these issues for years and isn't afraid to comment on uncomfortable issues. She is concerned that some women have stopped being supportive of other women and is keen to find ways to talk about this. 'If you're bigger, if you're older, if you're feeling vulnerable, if you're a learner, you can be treated badly. I think the girls who turn up in groups and support each other in their group are awesome, but I think they create new forms of exclusion.'

REBECCA

As with any major cultural shift, individuals can contribute to change. In surfing this can be done by watching the interplay in the line-up and helping to make it a welcoming space for everyone. For such a beautiful and meditative pastime, it is fraught with politics and complexities. A surf where a person feels excluded for any reason can lead to depletion and exhaustion. Being kind to people who are learning in the line-up helps. 'There's some kind of unspoken apprenticeship where you have to do the time as a beginner surfer. Why not just let someone have a wave? You don't own it. That's what we call it, right? This wave is mine. It's a wave. It's a piece of energy coming through water. It's not yours.'

City surfers, or weekend warriors as they are often called, who drive for a few hours on the weekend to surf can also receive some resistance in the line-up. Sometimes the city surfers are so excited to be surfing they ignore etiquette and drop in on other surfers. Sometimes the local surfers claim the break as their own and an endless stream of visitors throughout summer aren't welcome. Both parties can be at fault, but it is easy to forget that a weekend warrior has spent hours in a car to jump into the ocean for a surf they have waited all week for only to be growled at by a local who surfs daily. Bec understands that it's a real commitment when people travel from

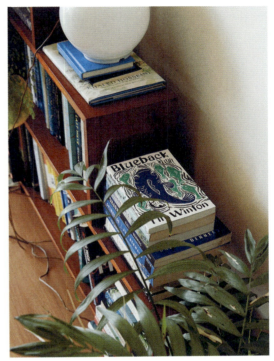

cities to the coast. 'These weekend warriors have to fight so hard to keep surfing in their life. I live in Brisbane so I'm one of them.'

For most of us surfing as a beginner can feel incredibly disheartening when comparing yourself to others in the line-up. A great surfer can make it look effortless, yet it takes hours of water time to get there. 'Don't worry if you're not the best surfer. Don't worry if you're not riding the green waves. Riding whitewash is fun, riding on your belly is fun, riding on your knees is fun. Enjoy it. Don't let someone else define what's right out in the water.'

Tips for a beginner surfer

—**Don't think you're too old**, the wrong body shape or not fit enough. The ocean is for everyone.

—**Try not to compare yourself** to others in the line-up. Surfing progression takes time

—**Don't worry about not getting waves**, enjoy the whole experience. You never regret a surf even if you just paddle around or have fun in the white wash.

—**Be patient!** Spend a good amount of time in the white water learning to stand up.

—**Learn on a foam board** – the bigger, the better. A large board enables you to catch loads of waves and the foam board doesn't hurt if it hits you when you fall off. They are readily available to hire at surf shops along the coast.

—**Have a surf lesson** at your local surf school. Teaching yourself is great fun but can also mean trying to undo bad habits later down the line.

—**Find a local meet-up** of surfing women who share waves, and join in. Or surf with a mate.

—**Learn surf etiquette** to avoid being scowled at or even yelled at in the line-up. If you think you may have done something wrong in the line-up, ask someone for tips. Surf etiquette is as much about safety as it is about promoting harmony.

—**Don't be shy!** Smile and say hello to people when you paddle out.

—**Sit on the beach** and watch surfers. If you see another surfer studying the line-up before they get in, ask them what they are looking at.

—**Surfboards are expensive**, so buy second-hand. If the board isn't for you, you can sell it on and try another shape. Don't be stingy when it comes to your boards, or think that you're not a good enough surfer to invest in a board shaped for you. You are good enough and it will accelerate your progression.

—**When you do join the line-up**, and start paddling into waves, it is just like crossing the road. Look left and right, and if it's clear go for it.

—**Be prepared to feel all the emotions.** It can be really frustrating and humiliating as a beginner, but persevere as the pay-off is worth it.

—**Research how to read the wind, swell and tides** by asking a friendly local for tips. If you've been a regular at the same spot for a while and they've seen you trying your best, they may be kind enough to give you pointers too.

—**Continue to get lessons** every now and then to have any bad habits corrected and learn more advanced techniques.

—**Be ready to compliment** someone in the line-up if you think their surfing looks amazing. Good vibes!

More information

One of the best parts about surfing is researching where to go. Here are some excellent suggestions for beginner waves in Australia and New Zealand to start you off:

New South Wales
Angourie
Yamba Main Beach

Queensland
First Point, Noosa
Greenmount Beach
Coolangatta
Caloundra, Sunshine Coast

South Australia
South Port, Adelaide
Christies Beach
Goolwa

Tasmania
Bicheno
Clifton Beach
Cloudy Bay, Bruny Island

Victoria
Point Leo
Anglesea Main Beach
Smiths Beach, Phillip Island

Western Australia
Mahomet's, Geraldton
Cottesloe Beach, Perth
Middleton Beach, Albany

New Zealand
Raglan, Waikato
Sumner Beach, Christchurch
Whangamatā, Coromandel

Thank you to featured surfers:

Angela
@southcoast_surfboards
southcoastsurfboards.com

Anna
@anna.skermer

Belinda
@belindabaggs
surfersforclimate.org.au

Beth
@waterclosetsurf

Daphne
@hiatus_daph

Ella
@ella_frances

Emma
@uandilabel

Gill
@shapedbyshe
shapedbyshe.com

Heidi
@heidiobrienart

Jess
@jessleitmanis
jessicaleitmanis.com

Jess
@killerwatts

Jessi
@jessirebel_art
jessirebelart.com.au

Jude
@zen_issa

Julia
bismarckhouse.com.au

Kate
@malrbu73

Kerry
@komylomy

Kirra
@kirramolnar

Lauren
@theseakin
laurenhill.com

Lizzie
@lizzie_stokely
lunajewellerybruny.com

Lucy
@saltwaterpilgram
equalpayforequalplay.com.au

Poppy
@tallpoppy__
tallpoppy.surf

Rebecca
@moving_oceans

Stevey
@steveyleeginger

Sue
surfdancer.com

Tia
@tia_mandu

Zoe
@zoe__makes
zoe-grey.com

Zana
@zanawright
zanawright.com

Authors

Thank you to our publisher, Kirsten Abbott, for your unwavering confidence in the book, which kept us going through the creative ups and downs and the lockdowns stopping and starting. Thanks to Fay and Brigid for your editing expertise and Akiko for the design.

I'm so stoked to have a friend in Willem who pitched the idea of working together back in 2013 when I wouldn't shut up about the tacky representation of female surfing in the marketing of some brands.

Thank you to Rebecca Olive, who has always been such a supporter of my surf writing, even back in the good old blogging days when it felt like every surf writer on the internet knew each other.

I had two writer friends who read drafts, so thank you Susie Quillinan and Favel Parrett for your encouragement. Also thank you to my other writing friends for the helpful tips when I was confronted with a blank page: Alice Addison, Cyn Sear and Samone Amba.

To the surfers at my home breaks: Kate, Kerry, Sam, John, Duncan, Jack and Andy. I love the carpark chats. Thanks to my fellow book lovers and co-workers at the bookshop – Chloe, Lucy, Carol, Ella, Nick, James and Lynne.

Thanks to the friends who listened to me bang on about the rollercoaster ride of writing my first book: George, Leo, Sarah, Laura, Daph, Dave, Ludo, Kat, Anna, Simon, Alex, Amanda, Ali, Chloe, Jade and Karen.

Thanks to Laura and James in Tassie and Sue and Pete in Byron for welcoming Rex and me into your homes while we worked on the book. Also to Chloe S, Cyn and Al for looking after my furry daughter. Thanks to Jay for the excellent co-parenting and to the Phangs for showing Rex a good time while I was busy.

Thanks to my parents. Without their generosity – giving me the deposit to buy my humble surf shack back in 2012 – none of this would have happened. Thank you to my siblings, Sue, Paul, Michael and Louise, for your unwavering support.

Thanks to Willem, Maddog and Al encouraging me to paddle into 'huge' three foot waves years ago. Thanks to the Baberahams, a small gang of lady surfers. We lived to get radical!

To every woman I've met during the making of this book, thank you for taking the time to share your stories about surfing.

Finally to my son, Rex. I love watching you fall in love with surfing and can't wait to share a party wave with you.

Gill Hutchison

I want to thank Kirsten Abbott for believing in our vision and working with us through all the lockdowns and limitations over the past two years. Thank you to the team at Thames and Hudson: Fay for the editing and Akiko for the design of this beautiful book.

I want to thank all the women who helped us by being part of this wonderful journey, some of whom are not showcased in these pages. You really challenged me out of my comfort zone and I'm forever grateful for the nudge you gave me when I was in doubt. I will keep these memories and new-built strength forever.

I would like to thank my friends and family for always supporting us and encouraging us to keep pushing forward. I'd like to thank Sarah Sproule for all the help over the past seven years, especially when Gill and I just started dabbling in the project. I will never forget the hours you spent on the beach, helping me pack gear while encouraging me the night before going on yet another trip, and caring for our son while I was away on a shoot. Thanks to my beautiful boy, Etienne, for always giving me purpose and making me feel like a cool dad. You're the light of my life.

Most importantly, my biggest thanks is to my teammate and friend Gill Hutchison for doing such a killer job on producing and writing our first book together. I've had so much fun working with you as a friend and colleague. I'm so impressed with who you have become since you started this project. I can't wait for the next one.

Lastly, after seeing a speech by Snoop Dogg, I would like to thank myself for feeling the fear and doing it anyway, driving thousands of kilometres, jumping off cliffs into monstrous surf, getting mauled by the ocean on rocks, swimming with sharks, pushing through very little sleep to catch yet another sunrise, for always saying yes when I really wished I could say no.

Willem-Dirk du Toit

Gill worked in the publishing industry for over ten years and when surfing took hold, she left the publishing world in the city to pursue a dream of life by the sea. Gill loves a chat in the surf carpark almost as much as surfing itself. In 2012 she bought a 1960s shack and after a short stint working in the surf industry landed her dream job in a bookshop. She lives on the Surf Coast with her son, Rex, and their dog, Betty.

gillhutchison.com
@babes_on_waves

Willem's father handed him a camera at the age of twelve and from there began a lifelong passion for photography. Growing up in South Africa he spent his holidays as a teen hitchhiking to his favourite surf spots. His desire for travel took him to London for three years in his early twenties. A yearning for more adventure launched a round the world trip from London that brought him to Australia in 2006, where he has lived ever since. Willem runs a successful architecture photography practice in Melbourne. He is constantly checking the surf forecast and will jump in his van any chance he can to find a wave. He lives in Melbourne with his young son, Etienne.

willem-dirk.com
@willem_dirk

First published in Australia in 2022
by Thames & Hudson Australia Pty Ltd
11 Central Boulevard, Portside Business Park
Port Melbourne, Victoria 3207
ABN: 72 004 751 964

First published in the United Kingdom in 2023
By Thames & Hudson Ltd
181a High Holborn
London WC1V 7QX

First published in the United States of America in 2023
By Thames & Hudson Inc.
500 Fifth Avenue
New York, New York 10110

Surf Life © Thames & Hudson Australia 2022

Text © Gill Hutchison 2022
Images © Willem-Dirk du Toit 2022
Front endpapers and pages 8–9 are reproduced
with thanks to U&I uandilabel.com.au

25 24 23 22   5 4 3 2 1

Thames & Hudson Australia wishes to acknowledge
that Aboriginal and Torres Strait Islander people are
the first storytellers of this nation and the traditional
custodians of the land on which we live and work. We
acknowledge their continuing culture and pay respect
to Elders past, present and future.

ISBN 978-1-760-76108-0
ISBN 978-1-760-76323-7 (U.S. edition)

A catalogue record for this
book is available from the
National Library of Australia

British Library Cataloguing-in-Publication Data
A catalogue record for this book is available from
the British Library

Library of Congress Control Number 2022937241

Every effort has been made to trace accurate
ownership of copyrighted text and visual materials
used in this book. Errors or omissions will be corrected
in subsequent editions, provided notification is sent to
the publisher.

Design: Akiko Chan
Editing: Bridget James
Typefaces: Lapidar by Dinamo
GT Ultra Fine by Grilli Type
Printed and bound in China by
C&C Offset Printing Co., Ltd

FSC® is dedicated to the promotion of responsible
forest management worldwide. This book is made
of material from FSC®-certified forests and other
controlled sources.

Be the first to know about our new releases,
exclusive content and author events by visiting
thamesandhudson.com.au
thamesandhudson.com
thamesandhudsonusa.com